CYBERSECURITY 101: A BEGINNER'S GUIDE TO UNDERSTANDING CYBER THREATS

PROTECTING YOUR DIGITAL ASSETS

PRAVIN BHAVSAR

Made with ♥ on the Notion Press Platform
www.notionpress.com

Contents

Preface

As we continue to rely more and more on technology to conduct our daily activities, the threat of cyber-attacks becomes increasingly prevalent. From personal information theft to corporate espionage, cyber security has become a critical aspect of modern life. This book aims to provide a comprehensive overview of the field of cyber security, covering topics such as the different types of cyber security threats, major cyber incidents, and key components of a cyber security framework for effective protection.

The book is divided into eight chapters, each of which covers a different aspect of cyber security. Chapter one provides an introduction to cyber security, discussing the CIA Triad, types of cyber security threats, and major cyber incidents. Chapter two covers cyber security frameworks, including popular frameworks such as the NIST Cybersecurity Framework and ISO 27001. Chapter three delves into cyber security risk assessment and management, including identifying risks and risk assessment methodologies.

Chapter four focuses on network security, discussing key technologies such as firewalls and intrusion prevention and detection systems. Chapter five covers application and mobile security, including common threats and best practices for securing applications. Chapter six discusses identity and access management, including IAM architecture and policies and procedures. Chapter seven covers incident response and management, including incident response frameworks and legal and regulatory considerations.

Finally, chapter eight addresses cybersecurity awareness and training, including building a cybersecurity awareness and training program and continuous learning and improvement. This book aims to provide readers with a comprehensive understanding of the field of cyber security, including the latest threats and best practices for protection.

I

An Introduction to Cyber Security

Introduction

The term "cyber security" refers to the practice of protecting computer systems, networks, and digital information from unauthorized access, theft, or damage. As our world becomes increasingly digitized, cyber security has become an essential component of protecting individuals, businesses, and governments from cyber threats.

Cyber threats can take many forms, including viruses, worms, Trojan horses, spyware, phishing attacks, ransomware, and denial-of-service attacks. These threats can result in data breaches, identity theft, financial losses, and even physical harm.

The impact of cyber-attacks can be significant. For individuals, cyber-attacks can result in the loss of personal information, financial loss, and damage to reputation. For businesses, cyber-attacks can lead to intellectual property theft, financial losses, and damage to customer trust. For governments, cyber-attacks can result in national security threats and the compromise of sensitive information.

As the reliance on technology continues to increase, so does the need for effective cyber security measures. This includes the implementation of strong passwords, multi-factor authentication, regular software updates, and the use of firewalls and antivirus software. It also involves educating users about safe online practices and the importance of staying vigilant against cyber threats.

Cyber Security and Information Security

Cybersecurity and Information security are closely related concepts, but they differ in terms of their scope and focus.

Information security refers to the protection of all forms of information, including physical and digital, from unauthorized access, use, disclosure, disruption, modification, or destruction. It encompasses the protection of all types of information, such as personal data, confidential business information, trade secrets, and intellectual property, regardless of the format in which it is stored or transmitted.

Cybersecurity, on the other hand, is a subset of information security that specifically addresses the protection of internet-connected systems, including hardware, software, and data, from cyber threats. It focuses on safeguarding digital devices, networks, and data from cyber-attacks, such as hacking, malware, phishing, social engineering, and denial of service attacks.

In other words, information security covers all types of information, while cybersecurity specifically addresses the protection of information and systems from cyber threats. However, both information security and cybersecurity are important aspects of protecting an organization's assets and ensuring its overall security posture.

Confidentiality, Integrity and Availability (CIA) Triad

The CIA triad is a widely used model for information security. It consists of three key concepts: confidentiality, integrity, and availability. The CIA triad provides a framework for evaluating and implementing information security measures to protect data and information systems. In this chapter, we will discuss each component of the CIA triad in detail.

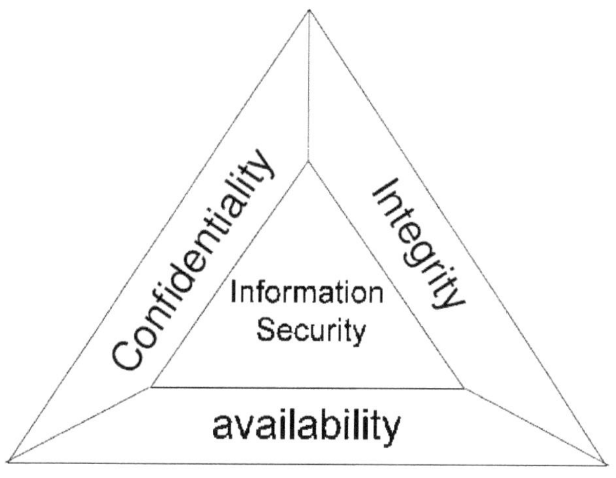

CIA TRIAD

Image 1: CIA TRIAD

Confidentiality: Confidentiality refers to the protection of sensitive information from unauthorized access, disclosure, or theft. Confidentiality ensures that only authorized individuals or systems can access or view sensitive data. Confidentiality is essential for protecting personal, financial, and business information, such as credit card numbers, medical records, trade secrets, and confidential customer data. Confidentiality can be achieved through various security measures such as access control, encryption, and data masking.

Access control limits access to information by implementing authentication and authorization measures, such as user identification and password protection. Encryption is another commonly used technique for ensuring confidentiality. Encryption is the process of converting plaintext information into ciphertext, which can only be decrypted with a specific key. Data masking is a technique that obscures sensitive data by replacing it with non-sensitive data or symbols.

Integrity: Integrity refers to the assurance that data and information are accurate, consistent, and complete. Integrity ensures that data has not been tampered with, modified, or altered without authorization. Integrity is critical for maintaining the trustworthiness of data and information systems. Data integrity can be ensured through various measures, such as data validation, access control, and backups.

Data validation ensures that data is entered accurately and consistently by implementing rules and constraints on data entry. Access control limits access to data and ensures that only authorized individuals can modify data. Backups provide an essential layer of protection against data loss due to system failures, cyberattacks, or natural disasters.

Availability: Availability refers to the ability of information systems and data to be accessible and usable when needed. Availability ensures that data and information systems are always available to authorized users. Availability is critical for maintaining business operations, customer service, and overall productivity. Availability can be ensured through various measures, such as redundant systems, disaster recovery plans, and backups.

Redundant systems ensure that critical systems and data are replicated in multiple locations to ensure availability in case of system failures. Disaster recovery plans provide a roadmap for restoring systems and data in case of natural disasters, cyberattacks, or other unexpected events. Backups provide a safety net for data and information systems by ensuring that critical data can be recovered in case of data loss or corruption.

In conclusion, the CIA triad provides a comprehensive framework for evaluating and implementing information security measures. Each component of the CIA triad plays a critical role in ensuring the confidentiality, integrity, and availability of data and information systems. By understanding and implementing the principles of the CIA triad, organizations can ensure that their information systems and data are secure and reliable.

Types of Cyber Security Threats

- **Malware:** Malware is a type of software that is designed to harm or disrupt computer systems. This can include viruses, worms, Trojan horses, and ransomware.

For example, a ransomware attack might infect a computer with software that encrypts all of the files on the system, rendering them inaccessible to the user unless a ransom is paid.

- **Phishing:** Phishing is a form of social engineering where attackers use email, text messages, or fake websites to trick individuals into providing sensitive information, such as login credentials or credit card numbers.

An example of a phishing attack might be an email that appears to be from a legitimate source, such as a bank or other financial institution, asking the recipient to click on a link and enter their login credentials.

- **Distributed Denial of Service (DDoS) Attacks:** A DDoS attack is an attempt to disrupt the normal functioning of a website or network by flooding it with traffic from multiple sources.

For example, an online retailer might be targeted with a DDoS attack during a major shopping event, causing their website to crash and preventing customers from making purchases.

- **Advanced Persistent Threats (APTs):** APTs are a type of cyber attack that is typically carried out by highly skilled and well-funded attackers. These attacks are designed to remain undetected for long periods of time, and the attackers often use multiple stages to achieve their objectives.

An example of an APT might be an attacker who gains access to an organization's network and spends months or even years gathering sensitive information before being detected.

- **Insider Threats:** Insider threats are threats posed by individuals within an organization who have access to sensitive information and may intentionally or unintentionally cause harm to the organization.

An example of an insider threat might be an employee who steals confidential business information and sells it to a competitor.

- **Zero-day Exploits:** A zero-day exploit is a type of cyber attack that takes advantage of a software vulnerability that is not yet known to the software vendor.

For example, an attacker might discover a vulnerability in a popular web browser and use it to install malware on a victim's computer before the vendor has a chance to patch the vulnerability.

- **Man-in-the-middle (MITM) Attacks:** A MITM attack is a type of attack where an attacker intercepts communication between two parties and can eavesdrop, modify, or inject messages into the communication.

For example, an attacker might intercept the communication between a user and their bank's website and steal the user's login credentials.

- **Password Attacks:** Password attacks are attempts to gain unauthorized access to a system by guessing or cracking a user's password.

For example, an attacker might use a brute-force attack to guess a user's password by trying every possible combination of characters until the correct password is found.

- **SQL Injection Attacks:** SQL injection attacks are attacks on databases, where attackers use malicious code to exploit vulnerabilities in the database and gain unauthorized access.

For example, an attacker might use an SQL injection attack to extract sensitive information from a database, such as usernames and passwords.

- **Internet of Things (IoT) Attacks:** IoT attacks involve exploiting vulnerabilities in IoT devices, such as smart home devices, to gain unauthorized access to networks or steal sensitive information.

For example, an attacker might exploit a vulnerability in a smart home device to gain access to the network and steal sensitive information, such as credit card numbers.

Major Cyber Incidents

- SolarWinds supply chain attack (2020): In December 2020, it was revealed that a group of hackers had gained access to the SolarWinds Orion software supply chain, allowing them to distribute a malware-infected software update to SolarWinds' customers. The malware, called

Sunburst, allowed the attackers to gain access to the networks of numerous government agencies and companies, including the US Treasury, the Department of Homeland Security, and Microsoft.

- Capital One data breach (2019): In July 2019, Capital One announced that a hacker had gained access to the personal information of over 100 million customers and applicants. The breach was caused by a misconfigured firewall that allowed the attacker to gain access to a web application firewall and subsequently access the data stored on Capital One's servers.
- WannaCry ransomware attack (2017): In May 2017, the WannaCry ransomware attacked spread rapidly across the world, affecting over 200,000 computers in 150 countries. The attack exploited a vulnerability in older versions of Microsoft Windows and encrypted users' files, demanding payment in Bitcoin in exchange for a decryption key.
- Equifax data breach (2017): In September 2017, credit reporting agency Equifax announced that a hacker had gained access to the personal information of 143 million customers, including names, birthdates, social security numbers, and addresses. The breach was caused by a vulnerability in Equifax's website software that was not patched in a timely manner.
- Yahoo data breaches (2013-2014): In 2016, Yahoo announced that it had been the victim of two separate data breaches in 2013 and 2014, affecting a total of 1.5 billion user accounts. The breaches included names, email addresses, birthdates, and hashed passwords. The company initially believed that the breaches were carried out by state-sponsored attackers.
- Marriott International data breach (2018): In November 2018, Marriott International announced that a hacker had gained access to the personal information of up to 500 million guests. The breach was caused by a vulnerability in the company's Starwood reservation system, which had been in place since 2014.
- Uber data breach (2016): In November 2017, ride-sharing company Uber announced that a 2016 data breach had affected 57 million customers and drivers. The breach was caused by hackers gaining access to a GitHub repository used by Uber developers, where they found login credentials for an Amazon Web Services account containing the data.
- Anthem data breach (2015): In February 2015, health insurance company Anthem announced that a hacker had gained access to the personal information of 80 million customers and employees, including names,

social security numbers, birthdates, and addresses. The breach was caused by a spear-phishing attack on an employee.

- Target data breach (2013): In December 2013, retail giant Target announced that a hacker had gained access to the personal information of 40 million customers, including credit and debit card information. The breach was caused by malware installed on Target's point-of-sale systems.
- Dyn DDoS attack (2016): In October 2016, a distributed denial-of-service (DDoS) attack affected internet infrastructure company Dyn, causing widespread internet disruptions across the United States and Europe. The attack was carried out using a botnet of Internet of Things (IoT) devices infected with the Mirai malware.

Key Components of Cyber Security Framework for Effective Protection

Cyber security comprises various essential components, such as:

- **Security policies and procedures:** Establishing a comprehensive set of security policies and procedures is essential to ensuring the security of an organization's information systems. These policies should cover areas such as access control, incident response, data backup and recovery, and employee security awareness training.
- **Network security:** This involves implementing security measures to protect an organization's networks from unauthorized access or attacks, including firewalls, intrusion detection and prevention systems, and virtual private networks (VPNs).
- **Application security:** This involves securing the software applications used by an organization, including web applications, mobile apps, and desktop applications. This includes measures such as secure coding practices, regular software updates, and vulnerability testing.
- **Identity and access management:** This involves controlling access to an organization's systems and data, ensuring that only authorized users have access. This can be achieved through measures such as strong authentication, access controls, and user activity monitoring.
- **Data security:** This involves protecting an organization's sensitive data, both in transit and at rest. This includes measures such as encryption,

data masking, and data loss prevention (DLP) systems.

- **Incident response:** This involves having a plan in place to respond to cyber security incidents, including procedures for identifying and containing the incident, notifying stakeholders, and recovering from the incident.
- **Physical security:** This involves securing an organization's physical assets, such as servers and data centers, from unauthorized access or theft.
- **Security monitoring and analysis:** This involves monitoring an organization's systems and networks for suspicious activity, and analyzing security events to identify potential threats or vulnerabilities.
- **Training and awareness:** Ensuring that employees are aware of the organization's security policies and procedures, and trained to identify and respond to potential security threats, is a crucial component of cyber security.

These components work together to create a comprehensive cyber security framework that can help organizations protect against a wide range of cyber threats.

Understanding Cyber Security Governance: Components and Importance

Cyber security governance is the system of policies, processes, and procedures that an organization uses to manage and oversee its cyber security program. It is an essential component of effective cyber security, as it helps to ensure that an organization's security strategy aligns with its business objectives and that the necessary resources are in place to achieve those objectives.

Effective cyber security governance typically includes the following elements:

- **Cyber security strategy:** This involves developing a comprehensive strategy for managing an organization's cyber security risks, including establishing priorities, identifying potential threats and vulnerabilities, and implementing appropriate controls.
- **Risk management:** This involves identifying, assessing, and managing cyber security risks across the organization, including through risk

assessments, vulnerability testing, and incident response planning.

- **Compliance:** This involves ensuring that an organization's cyber security program meets all applicable legal and regulatory requirements, as well as industry standards and best practices.
- **Resource management:** This involves allocating the necessary resources, including funding, personnel, and technology, to support an organization's cyber security program.
- **Performance measurement:** This involves establishing metrics and performance indicators to measure the effectiveness of an organization's cyber security program and identify areas for improvement.
- **Incident response planning:** This involves establishing procedures for responding to cyber security incidents, including identifying the incident, containing it, and recovering from it.

Effective cyber security governance requires collaboration and communication across all levels of an organization, from the board of directors to front-line employees. By establishing a strong governance framework, organizations can help to ensure the security and resilience of their information systems and protect against cyber threats.

Conclusion

Cyber security is a crucial aspect of modern society, as the increasing reliance on technology has led to a rise in cyber threats. To effectively protect against these threats, organizations must implement a comprehensive cyber security program that includes policies, procedures, and technologies to secure their networks, systems, and data. This program should be based on a strong governance framework that aligns with the organization's business objectives and meets all applicable legal and regulatory requirements. The key components of a cyber security program include security policies and procedures, network and application security, identity and access management, data security, incident response, physical security, security monitoring and analysis, and training and awareness. By understanding these components and implementing a comprehensive cyber security program, organizations can effectively protect against cyber threats and ensure the security and resilience of their information systems.

II

Frameworks for Cybersecurity

Introduction

As we have seen in the previous chapter, cyber security is a complex and multifaceted discipline that requires a comprehensive approach to be effective. To help organizations build a structured and consistent cyber security program, various cyber security frameworks have been developed. These frameworks provide a set of guidelines, best practices, and standards for securing an organization's networks, systems, and data.

In this chapter, we will explore some of the most popular cyber security frameworks that organizations can use to build their cyber security program. We will provide an overview of each framework, including its objectives, key components, and how it can be applied in practice. We will also discuss the benefits of using a cyber security framework, and some of the challenges that organizations may face when implementing one.

By understanding the different cyber security frameworks available, organizations can select the framework that best meets their needs and requirements, and use it as a blueprint for building a robust and effective cyber security program.

Cyber Security Frameworks

Cybersecurity frameworks provide a structured approach to managing cybersecurity risks, enabling organizations to identify, assess, and manage cybersecurity risks more effectively. In this chapter, we will explore some of the most widely used cybersecurity frameworks and their key features.

What is a Cybersecurity Framework?

A cybersecurity framework is a set of guidelines, best practices, and standards that organizations can use to manage cybersecurity risks effectively. These frameworks provide a structured approach to cybersecurity risk management, enabling organizations to identify, assess, and manage cybersecurity risks more effectively.

Why are Cybersecurity Frameworks Important?

Cybersecurity frameworks are important for several reasons. First, they provide a structured approach to cybersecurity risk management, enabling organizations to identify and assess cybersecurity risks more effectively. Second, they help organizations to establish and maintain a cybersecurity risk management program that is aligned with industry best practices and standards. Finally, they help organizations to achieve compliance with cybersecurity regulations and standards, such as the General Data Protection Regulation (GDPR) and the Payment Card Industry Data Security Standard (PCI DSS).

Popular Cybersecurity Frameworks

There are several cybersecurity frameworks in use today. In this section, we will explore some of the most widely used frameworks and their key features.

NIST Cybersecurity Framework

The National Institute of Standards and Technology (NIST) Cybersecurity Framework is one of the most widely used cybersecurity frameworks. It provides a set of guidelines and best practices for organizations to manage and reduce cybersecurity risks. The framework is organized into five core functions: Identify, Protect, Detect, Respond, and Recover. These core functions help organizations to manage cybersecurity risks in a structured and comprehensive manner.

ISO 27001

The ISO 27001 standard provides a set of requirements for establishing, implementing, maintaining, and continuously improving an Information Security Management System (ISMS). The standard is designed to help organizations manage and protect their sensitive information using a risk management approach. The standard is organized into several sections, including risk assessment, security controls, and management commitment.

CIS Controls

The Center for Internet Security (CIS) Controls is a set of guidelines and best practices for cybersecurity risk management. The controls are organized into 20 categories, covering areas such as inventory and control of hardware assets, continuous vulnerability management, and secure configuration for hardware and software. The CIS Controls provide a comprehensive approach to cybersecurity risk management, enabling organizations to manage risks effectively.

COBIT

COBIT (Control Objectives for Information and Related Technology) is a framework developed by ISACA (Information Systems Audit and Control Association) for IT governance and management. The framework is designed to help organizations align their IT strategy with their business objectives and manage risks effectively. The COBIT framework is organized into several sections, including governance and management, delivery and support, and monitoring and evaluation.

NIST Cybersecurity Framework

The NIST Cybersecurity Framework is a widely used framework for managing cybersecurity risks. It was developed by the National Institute of Standards and Technology (NIST) in response to a 2013 executive order from former US President Barack Obama. The framework provides a set of guidelines, best practices, and standards for organizations to manage and reduce cybersecurity risks.

The NIST Cybersecurity Framework is built around five core functions: Identify, Protect, Detect, Respond, and Recover. These functions are designed to provide a comprehensive approach to cybersecurity risk management.

1. **Identify**

The Identify function is focused on understanding the organization's assets, risks, and vulnerabilities. It involves identifying the organization's cybersecurity risks, the systems and assets that need to be protected, and the dependencies between these assets. The Identify function is crucial for developing an effective cybersecurity risk management strategy.

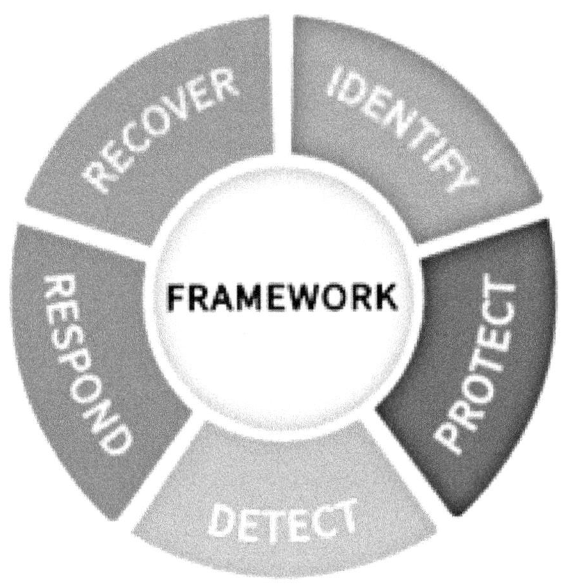

NIST FRAMEWORK

Image 2 : NIST Framework

2. **Protect**

The Protect function is focused on implementing safeguards to prevent or limit the impact of a cybersecurity attack. It involves implementing security controls such as access controls, firewalls, and encryption to protect the organization's assets. The Protect function is designed to help organizations establish a strong cybersecurity posture.

3. **Detect**

The Detect function is focused on identifying cybersecurity events and incidents as quickly as possible. It involves implementing mechanisms such as intrusion detection systems, security information and event management (SIEM) systems, and anomaly detection systems to detect cybersecurity events. The Detect function is designed to help organizations detect cybersecurity incidents early and respond more effectively.

4. **Respond**

The Respond function is focused on responding to cybersecurity incidents promptly and effectively. It involves developing and implementing an incident response plan that outlines the steps to be taken in the event of a cybersecurity incident. The Respond function is designed to help organizations minimize the impact of cybersecurity incidents and quickly restore normal operations.

5. **Recover**

The Recover function is focused on restoring normal operations as quickly as possible after a cybersecurity incident. It involves developing and implementing a business continuity plan that outlines the steps to be taken to recover from a cybersecurity incident. The Recover function is designed to help organizations minimize the impact of cybersecurity incidents and quickly return to normal operations.

The NIST Cybersecurity Framework also includes a set of implementation tiers that help organizations to gauge their cybersecurity risk management maturity. These tiers range from Partial to Adaptive and are designed to help organizations understand their current cybersecurity risk management capabilities and identify areas for improvement.

The NIST Cybersecurity Framework is a comprehensive framework for managing cybersecurity risks. Its five core functions provide a structured approach to cybersecurity risk management, enabling organizations to identify, assess, and manage cybersecurity risks more effectively. The framework's implementation tiers help organizations to gauge their cybersecurity risk management maturity and identify areas for improvement.

ISO 27001

ISO 27001 is a global standard for Information Security Management Systems (ISMS) that provides a comprehensive framework for managing and protecting sensitive information. It specifies the requirements for establishing, implementing, maintaining, and continually improving an ISMS.

The purpose of ISO 27001 is to help organizations establish and maintain effective security controls to protect their sensitive information from unauthorized access, modification, disclosure, or destruction. The standard is designed to be applicable to organizations of all sizes and types, and can be applied to any industry sector.

ISO 27001 is based on the Plan-Do-Check-Act (PDCA) cycle, a model for continuous improvement. The standard consists of 10 sections, each of which covers a specific area of information security management.

1. **Scope**

The scope of the standard should be clearly defined and documented, including the types of information that the ISMS will protect.

2. **Normative references**

This section lists the reference standards and guidelines that are relevant to the implementation of ISO 27001.

3. **Terms and definitions**

This section provides definitions of the terms used in the standard.

4. **Context of the organization**

This section requires organizations to understand the internal and external context in which they operate, including the needs and expectations of interested parties.

5. **Leadership**

This section requires top management to demonstrate their commitment to information security and to provide adequate resources for the implementation of the ISMS.

6. **Planning**

This section requires organizations to develop a risk management plan, which includes risk assessment, risk treatment, and the selection of security controls.

7. **Support**

This section requires organizations to provide adequate resources, competencies, and communication channels to support the implementation of the ISMS.

8. **Operation**

This section requires organizations to implement the risk treatment plan, including the selection of security controls, the implementation of security measures, and the operation of the ISMS.

9. **Performance evaluation**

This section requires organizations to monitor and measure the performance of the ISMS, including the effectiveness of the security controls and the achievement of objectives.

10. **Improvement**

This section requires organizations to continually improve the effectiveness of the ISMS, including the identification and correction of nonconformities and the implementation of preventive actions.

To achieve ISO 27001 certification, an organization must undergo a rigorous external audit by an accredited certification body. The audit assesses the organization's compliance with the requirements of the standard and its effectiveness in managing information security risks.

ISO 27001 is a globally recognized standard for Information Security Management Systems. Its requirements cover all aspects of information security management, including risk assessment, risk treatment, and the selection and implementation of security controls. By implementing ISO 27001, organizations can effectively manage and protect their sensitive information, demonstrate their commitment to information security, and comply with legal and regulatory requirements.

Center For Information Security (CIS) Controls

CIS Controls, also known as the Center for Internet Security Controls, is a set of best practices for cybersecurity that organizations can use to improve their security posture. The CIS Controls were developed by a consortium of cybersecurity experts, and they are based on real-world attacks and breaches. The controls provide a prioritized and actionable list of actions that organizations can take to mitigate the most common and damaging cyber threats.

The CIS Controls are divided into three categories:

1. **Basic Controls**

The basic controls are the foundational security measures that all organizations should implement. These controls include inventory and control of hardware assets, inventory and control of software assets, continuous vulnerability management, controlled use of administrative privileges, and secure configuration for hardware and software on mobile devices, laptops, workstations, and servers.

2. **Foundational Controls**

The foundational controls build on the basic controls and are designed to provide additional protection against cyber threats. These controls include email and web browser protections, malware defenses, data recovery capabilities, security skills assessment and appropriate training to fill gaps, and application software security.

3. **Organizational Controls**

The organizational controls are designed to ensure that the organization has the policies, processes, and resources in place to effectively manage cybersecurity risks. These controls include a security awareness and training program, a security audit log, controlled access based on the need to know, account monitoring and control, and a secure network engineering.

The CIS Controls are flexible and can be customized to meet the specific needs of an organization. Organizations can use the controls as a roadmap to improve their security posture over time, starting with the basic controls and building up to the more advanced foundational and organizational controls.

The CIS Controls are updated regularly to reflect the evolving cyber threat landscape. The latest version of the CIS Controls includes a total of 18 controls, each with specific sub-controls that organizations can implement to improve their security posture.

To help organizations implement the CIS Controls, the Center for Internet Security provides a variety of resources, including implementation guides, tools, and training. The CIS Controls can also be mapped to other cybersecurity frameworks, such as NIST, ISO 27001, and COBIT, to provide a comprehensive and integrated approach to cybersecurity.

COBIT Framework

COBIT (Control Objectives for Information and Related Technology) is a framework developed by the ISACA (Information Systems Audit and Control Association) to provide guidance on information technology (IT) governance and management. COBIT provides a comprehensive set of controls and best practices for IT management and governance, with the goal of ensuring the effective and efficient use of IT resources in support of business objectives.

COBIT consists of five main components:

1. **Framework:**

The COBIT framework defines the objectives, governance principles, and management practices for IT governance and management.

2. **Process Reference Model:**

The COBIT process reference model provides a set of best practices for IT management across four domains: plan and organize, acquire and implement, deliver and support, and monitor and evaluate.

3. **Control Objectives:**

COBIT includes a set of control objectives that are designed to help organizations meet their IT governance and management objectives. These control objectives are aligned with the process reference model and are organized by IT-related goals and objectives.

4. **Management Guidelines:**

COBIT provides management guidelines for implementing and managing IT governance and management processes, including guidance on implementing controls and managing risks.

5. **Audit Guidelines:**

COBIT includes audit guidelines for assessing the effectiveness of IT governance and management processes, including guidance on planning and conducting IT audits and reporting on findings.

Overall, COBIT helps organizations to establish a comprehensive IT governance and management framework that aligns with business objectives and supports effective and efficient use of IT resources. COBIT is widely used in organizations of all sizes and industries and can be customized to meet the specific needs and requirements of each organization.

PCI-DSS Standard

PCI-DSS (Payment Card Industry Data Security Standard) is a set of security standards designed to protect payment card data and ensure the secure handling of payment transactions. The standard is managed by the PCI Security Standards Council, which is made up of the major credit card companies such as Visa, MasterCard, American Express, and Discover.

The PCI-DSS framework consists of six main objectives and 12 requirements that organizations must meet in order to comply with the standard. These objectives and requirements are as follows:

1. **Build and Maintain a Secure Network**

Requirement 1: Install and maintain a firewall configuration to protect cardholder data.

Requirement 2: Do not use vendor-supplied defaults for system passwords and other security parameters.

2. **Protect Cardholder Data**

Requirement 3: Protect stored cardholder data.

Requirement 4: Encrypt transmission of cardholder data across open, public networks.

3. **Maintain a Vulnerability Management Program**

Requirement 5: Use and regularly update anti-virus software or programs.

Requirement 6: Develop and maintain secure systems and applications.

4. **Implement Strong Access Control Measures**

Requirement 7: Restrict access to cardholder data by business need-to-know.

Requirement 8: Assign a unique ID to each person with computer access.

Requirement 9: Restrict physical access to cardholder data.

5. **Regularly Monitor and Test Networks**

Requirement 10: Track and monitor all access to network resources and cardholder data.

Requirement 11: Regularly test security systems and processes.

6. **Maintain an Information Security Policy**

Requirement 12: Maintain a policy that addresses information security.

The PCI-DSS framework is a comprehensive set of security standards that help organizations to protect payment card data and ensure the secure handling of payment transactions. Compliance with the standard is mandatory for all organizations that handle payment card data, and failure to comply can result in significant financial penalties and reputational damage. Organizations that handle payment card data should work closely with their payment card providers and security experts to ensure that they meet the requirements of the PCI-DSS framework.

Conclusion

Cybersecurity frameworks are an essential component of modern-day cybersecurity risk management. They provide a structured approach to managing cybersecurity risks, enabling organizations to identify, assess, and manage risks more effectively. There are several popular cybersecurity frameworks in use today, each with its own set of guidelines, best practices, and standards. By implementing a cybersecurity framework, organizations can establish and maintain a robust cybersecurity risk management program that is aligned with industry best practices and standards.

III

Cyber Security Risk Assessment and Management

Introduction

Cyber threats are constantly evolving and becoming more sophisticated, making it crucial for organizations to take a proactive approach to cybersecurity risk assessment and management. This chapter

will introduce the concept of cybersecurity risk assessment and management, explaining what it is, why it is important, and how organizations can benefit from implementing a cybersecurity risk assessment and management program.

What is Cybersecurity Risk Assessment and Management?

Cybersecurity risk assessment and management is a process that involves identifying, assessing, and mitigating cybersecurity risks. This process is used to protect an organization's digital infrastructure from cyber threats, such as data breaches, system failures, and other security incidents.

The process of cybersecurity risk assessment and management involves the following steps:

1. **Identify Cybersecurity Risks:** This step involves identifying potential cybersecurity risks to an organization's digital infrastructure. These

risks can come from a variety of sources, including external threats like hackers and malware, as well as internal threats like employee errors and system failures.

2. **Assess Cybersecurity Risks:** Once cybersecurity risks have been identified, the next step is to assess their potential impact on the organization. This involves evaluating the likelihood and severity of the risk and determining how it could affect the organization's operations, assets, and reputation.
3. **Mitigate Cybersecurity Risks:** The final step is to develop and implement strategies to mitigate cybersecurity risks. This may involve implementing technical controls like firewalls and encryption, as well as administrative controls like policies and procedures to ensure that employees are following best practices.

Importance Cybersecurity Risk Assessment and Management

Cybersecurity risk assessment and management are essential for organizations of all sizes and industries for several reasons:

1. **Protecting Sensitive Data:** One of the primary goals of cybersecurity risk assessment and management is to protect an organization's sensitive data from cyber threats. This includes personal information, financial data, and intellectual property.
2. **Maintaining Business Continuity:** Cybersecurity incidents can cause significant disruptions to an organization's operations, leading to lost productivity and revenue. By identifying and mitigating cybersecurity risks, organizations can maintain business continuity and avoid costly downtime.
3. **Regulatory Compliance:** Many industries are subject to regulations that require organizations to implement cybersecurity measures to protect sensitive data. By implementing a cybersecurity risk assessment and management program, organizations can ensure that they are in compliance with these regulations.
4. **Protecting Reputation:** Cybersecurity incidents can damage an organization's reputation and erode customer trust. By implementing a cybersecurity risk assessment and management program, organizations can protect their reputation and maintain customer confidence.

Benefits of Implementing a Cybersecurity Risk Assessment and Management Program

Implementing a cybersecurity risk assessment and management program can provide several benefits to organizations, including:

1. **Improved Security:** By identifying and mitigating cybersecurity risks, organizations can improve their overall security posture, reducing the likelihood of cyber incidents.
2. **Cost Savings:** Cybersecurity incidents can be costly, both in terms of direct financial losses and indirect costs like lost productivity and damage to reputation. By implementing a cybersecurity risk assessment and management program, organizations can avoid these costs.
3. **Compliance:** Implementing a cybersecurity risk assessment and management program can help organizations comply with industry regulations and standards, avoiding potential fines and legal consequences.
4. **Competitive Advantage:** Organizations that can demonstrate a strong cybersecurity posture may have a competitive advantage, as customers and partners may be more likely to do business with them.

Identifying Cybersecurity Risks

The first step in implementing a cybersecurity risk assessment and management program is to identify potential cybersecurity risks to an organization's digital infrastructure.

Sources of Cybersecurity Risks

Cybersecurity risks can come from a variety of sources, including:

1. **External Threats:** These are threats from outside the organization, such as hackers, malware, and other cybercriminals.
2. **Internal Threats:** These are threats from within the organization, such as employee errors, system failures, and intentional actions by employees or contractors.
3. **Third-Party Risks:** These are risks associated with third-party vendors and contractors that have access to an organization's digital

infrastructure.

4. **Physical Threats:** These are risks associated with physical security, such as theft of hardware or unauthorized access to physical assets.
5. **Compliance Risks:** These are risks associated with non-compliance with industry regulations and standards.

Identifying Cybersecurity Risks

To effectively identify cybersecurity risks, organizations can follow a systematic approach, which includes the following steps:

1. **Asset Inventory:** The first step is to create an inventory of all the digital assets that an organization possesses, including hardware, software, and data.
2. **Threat Identification:** Once an inventory has been created, the next step is to identify potential threats to these assets. This may involve analyzing threat intelligence reports, reviewing historical incident data, and conducting vulnerability assessments.
3. **Vulnerability Assessment:** After potential threats have been identified, the next step is to conduct a vulnerability assessment to identify potential weaknesses in an organization's digital infrastructure. This may involve conducting vulnerability scans and penetration testing.
4. **Risk Analysis:** Once potential vulnerabilities have been identified, the next step is to assess the potential impact of these vulnerabilities on an organization's operations, assets, and reputation. This may involve conducting a risk analysis to evaluate the likelihood and severity of a potential incident.
5. **Risk Prioritization:** After conducting a risk analysis, the next step is to prioritize risks based on their potential impact on an organization's operations, assets, and reputation. This may involve assigning risk scores to each identified risk.
6. **Risk Mitigation:** The final step is to develop and implement strategies to mitigate identified cybersecurity risks. This may involve implementing technical controls like firewalls and encryption, as well as administrative controls like policies and procedures to ensure that employees are following best practices.

Tools and Techniques for Identifying Cybersecurity Risks

Organizations can use several tools and techniques to effectively identify cybersecurity risks, including:

1. **Threat Intelligence:** Threat intelligence involves collecting and analyzing information about potential cyber threats from a variety of sources, including open-source intelligence, social media, and the dark web.
2. **Vulnerability Scanning:** Vulnerability scanning involves using automated tools to scan an organization's digital infrastructure for known vulnerabilities.
3. **Penetration Testing:** Penetration testing involves simulating a cyber attack to identify potential vulnerabilities and weaknesses in an organization's digital infrastructure.

1. **Risk Assessment Frameworks:** Risk assessment frameworks, such as the National Institute of Standards and Technology (NIST) Cybersecurity Framework, provide guidelines for identifying and mitigating cybersecurity risks.

Risk Assessment Process

The risk assessment process involves the following steps:

1. **Asset Identification:** The first step is to identify the assets that are at risk. This includes hardware, software, data, and any other digital assets that are critical to an organization's operations.
2. **Threat Analysis:** The next step is to analyze potential threats to these assets. This may involve using threat intelligence, reviewing historical incident data, and conducting vulnerability assessments.
3. **Vulnerability Assessment:** Once potential threats have been identified, the next step is to conduct a vulnerability assessment to identify potential weaknesses in an organization's digital infrastructure. This may involve conducting vulnerability scans and penetration testing.

4. **Risk Analysis:** The next step is to analyze the potential impact of identified risks on an organization's operations, assets, and reputation. This may involve conducting a risk analysis to evaluate the likelihood and severity of a potential incident.
5. **Risk Evaluation:** The final step is to evaluate the level of risk posed by identified cybersecurity risks. This involves assigning a risk score or rating to each identified risk based on the potential impact and likelihood of occurrence.

Risk Assessment Methodologies

Organizations can use several methodologies to assess cybersecurity risks, including:

1. **Qualitative Risk Assessment:** This methodology involves assessing risks based on subjective judgments, such as the potential impact of a risk on an organization's operations, assets, and reputation. This method can be useful when data is limited, or when a quick assessment is required.
2. **Quantitative Risk Assessment:** This methodology involves using numerical data to assess risks, such as the probability of a risk occurring and the potential financial impact of an incident. This method can be more precise but may require more data and analysis.
3. **Hybrid Risk Assessment:** This methodology combines both qualitative and quantitative assessments to provide a more comprehensive analysis of potential risks.

Risk Assessment Tools

Organizations can use several tools to assess cybersecurity risks, including:

1. **Risk Assessment Frameworks:** Risk assessment frameworks, such as the National Institute of Standards and Technology (NIST) Cybersecurity Framework, provide guidelines for assessing and mitigating cybersecurity risks.

2. **Risk Assessment Software:** Risk assessment software can help automate the risk assessment process and provide a more comprehensive analysis of potential risks.
3. **Risk Assessment Templates:** Risk assessment templates provide a structured approach to assessing cybersecurity risks and can help ensure that all relevant risks are identified and evaluated.

Once potential cybersecurity risks have been identified and assessed, the next step in a cybersecurity risk assessment and management program is to manage these risks.

Risk Management Process

The risk management process involves the following steps:

1. **Risk Prioritization:** The first step in managing cybersecurity risks is to prioritize them based on their potential impact and likelihood of occurrence. This involves assigning a risk score or rating to each identified risk and developing a risk management plan based on these scores.
2. **Risk Mitigation:** The next step is to implement strategies to mitigate identified risks. This may involve implementing security controls, such as firewalls, antivirus software, and access controls, to prevent or reduce the impact of potential incidents.
3. **Risk Transfer:** Another option is to transfer the risk to a third-party, such as an insurance provider or a cloud service provider. This may involve purchasing cyber insurance or using a cloud provider with strong security measures in place.
4. **Risk Acceptance:** In some cases, organizations may choose to accept a certain level of risk if the cost of mitigation outweighs the potential impact of the risk.
5. **Risk Monitoring:** The final step is to monitor and review the effectiveness of implemented risk management strategies on an ongoing basis. This may involve conducting regular security audits and vulnerability assessments.

Risk mitigation strategies

The common risk mitigation strategies are:

1. **Risk Avoidance:** This involves avoiding activities or decisions that could potentially lead to risks.
2. **Risk Transfer:** This involves transferring the risk to a third party, such as an insurance company.
3. **Risk Reduction:** This involves taking actions to reduce the likelihood or impact of the risk.
4. **Risk Acceptance:** This involves accepting the risk and dealing with it if it occurs.

Risk Management Strategies

Organizations can use several strategies to manage cybersecurity risks, including:

1. **Defense-in-Depth:** This strategy involves implementing multiple layers of security controls to prevent or mitigate potential incidents. This may include using firewalls, intrusion detection systems, and access controls.
2. **Incident Response Planning:** Developing an incident response plan can help organizations respond quickly and effectively to potential incidents. This involves outlining the steps to take in the event of a cybersecurity incident, such as isolating affected systems and contacting law enforcement.
3. **Employee Training and Awareness:** Educating employees on cybersecurity best practices can help prevent incidents caused by human error, such as phishing attacks or data breaches caused by weak passwords.
4. **Continuous Monitoring:** Regularly monitoring an organization's digital infrastructure can help detect and respond to potential incidents quickly. This may involve using security information and event management (SIEM) tools or outsourcing to a managed security service provider (MSSP).

Cybersecurity Risk Assessment and Management Best Practices

Effective cybersecurity risk assessment and management requires a comprehensive and systematic approach.

Best practices for conducting a successful cybersecurity risk assessment and management program.

1. **Establish a Risk Management Framework:** Establishing a risk management framework is essential for effective cybersecurity risk assessment and management. This framework should include guidelines for risk identification, assessment, mitigation, monitoring, and reporting. It should also include roles and responsibilities for key stakeholders involved in the risk management process.
2. **Conduct Regular Risk Assessments:** Conducting regular risk assessments is critical for identifying and mitigating potential cybersecurity risks. Regular assessments can help organizations stay current with evolving threats and vulnerabilities, and identify any changes in their risk profile. Risk assessments should be conducted at least annually, and more frequently if there are significant changes to an organization's digital infrastructure or business operations.
3. **Involve Key Stakeholders:** Cybersecurity risk assessment and management is a team effort, and it is important to involve key stakeholders from across the organization. This may include executives, IT staff, security professionals, and legal and compliance personnel. By involving these stakeholders, organizations can ensure that all potential risks are identified and effectively managed.
4. **Implement Risk Mitigation Strategies:** Once risks have been identified and assessed, it is important to implement strategies to mitigate these risks. This may include implementing security controls, such as firewalls, intrusion detection systems, and access controls. It may also involve developing incident response plans and conducting regular security awareness training for employees.
5. **Regularly Monitor and Review Risk Management Strategies:** Cybersecurity risks are constantly evolving, and it is important to regularly monitor and review the effectiveness of implemented risk management strategies. This may involve conducting regular security audits and vulnerability assessments. Organizations should also

regularly review their risk management framework and make any necessary updates based on changing threats and business operations.

6. **Stay Current with Emerging Threats and Technologies:** As cybersecurity threats continue to evolve, it is important for organizations to stay current with emerging threats and technologies. This may involve attending industry conferences and staying up-to-date with cybersecurity news and trends. It may also involve partnering with cybersecurity vendors and experts to stay current with the latest security technologies and best practices.

Cybersecurity Risk Assessment and Management Tools

In addition to following best practices for cybersecurity risk assessment and management, organizations can also leverage various tools to enhance their risk management program such as:

1. **Vulnerability Scanners:** Vulnerability scanners are automated tools that can help organizations identify vulnerabilities in their digital infrastructure, such as outdated software or unpatched systems. These tools can help organizations prioritize their risk management efforts by identifying the most critical vulnerabilities that need to be addressed.
2. **Penetration Testing Tools:** Penetration testing tools simulate cyberattacks on an organization's digital infrastructure to identify potential vulnerabilities and weaknesses. These tools can help organizations better understand their risk profile and develop more effective risk mitigation strategies.
3. **Security Information and Event Management (SIEM) Systems:** SIEM systems collect and analyze data from various sources, including security logs, to identify potential security incidents. These systems can help organizations quickly detect and respond to potential cyber threats.
4. **Risk Assessment Software:** Risk assessment software can help organizations streamline their risk assessment and management processes by providing a centralized platform for identifying and tracking potential risks. These tools may include risk assessment templates, risk scoring algorithms, and reporting features.
5. **Compliance Management Tools:** Compliance management tools can help organizations ensure they are meeting regulatory and industry-

specific requirements related to cybersecurity. These tools may include compliance checklists, policy templates, and automated compliance reporting.

6. **Incident Response Tools:** Incident response tools can help organizations quickly respond to potential cybersecurity incidents. These tools may include automated incident response playbooks, incident response coordination software, and forensic analysis tools.

Conclusion

cybersecurity risk assessment and management are essential for organizations to protect their digital infrastructure and sensitive data from potential cyber threats. By following best practices for cybersecurity risk assessment and management, organizations can identify potential risks, develop effective risk mitigation strategies, and better detect and respond to potential security incidents. Effective cybersecurity risk assessment and management requires a comprehensive and systematic approach that involves regular risk assessments, stakeholder involvement, risk mitigation strategies, and ongoing monitoring and review. By following these best practices and leveraging the right tools, organizations can reduce their risk exposure and maintain the integrity of their digital infrastructure.

IV

Network Security: Protecting Your Organization's Digital Perimeter

Introduction

As organizations continue to embrace digital transformation, their networks have become the digital perimeters that protect their sensitive data and assets. With the increasing number of cyberattacks targeting networks, it's crucial to ensure that your organization's network security is robust and resilient. This chapter provides an overview of network security, its importance, and the key technologies and best practices that can help protect your organization's digital perimeter.

What is Network Security?

Network security is the practice of protecting computer networks from unauthorized access, misuse, modification, or destruction. It involves the use of hardware, software, and protocols to secure networks and their components, including devices, applications, and data. The goal of network security is to ensure that only authorized users have access to network resources and to prevent unauthorized users from gaining access or causing harm.

Importance of Network Security

Network security is crucial for protecting an organization's digital assets and ensuring business continuity. Here are some of the key reasons why network security is essential:

1. **Protects Confidential Data:** Network security helps prevent unauthorized access to confidential data, such as customer information, financial data, and intellectual property.
2. **Ensures Business Continuity:** Network security ensures that critical business functions and applications are available and accessible to authorized users, even during a cyber-attack or other disruptive event.
3. **Maintains Reputation:** A cyber-attack or data breach can damage an organization's reputation and lead to financial losses. Network security helps prevent such incidents and protects an organization's brand and reputation.
4. **Compliance:** Many regulatory standards and laws require organizations to implement network security measures to protect sensitive data and ensure compliance.

Key Technologies and Best Practices for Network Security

1. **Firewall:** A firewall is a network security device that monitors and controls incoming and outgoing network traffic based on predetermined security rules. Firewalls help prevent unauthorized access to networks and protect against malware and other cyber threats.
2. **Intrusion Detection and Prevention Systems (IDPS):** An IDPS is a security technology that monitors network traffic for signs of unauthorized access or attacks and takes action to prevent or mitigate them.
3. **Virtual Private Network (VPN):** A VPN is a secure connection between two or more networks that allows users to access network resources remotely. VPNs use encryption to protect network traffic from

eavesdropping and unauthorized access.

4. **Access Controls:** Access controls help ensure that only authorized users have access to network resources. This includes the use of passwords, multi-factor authentication, and role-based access controls.
5. **Network Segmentation:** Network segmentation involves dividing a network into smaller subnetworks or segments, each with its own security controls. This helps limit the impact of a cyber attack and prevents lateral movement by attackers.
6. **Patch Management:** Patch management is the process of identifying, testing, and applying software updates or patches to fix vulnerabilities in network devices and software.
7. **Security Information and Event Management (SIEM):** SIEM is a technology that aggregates and analyzes security events and alerts from various sources to identify potential security incidents.

Firewalls

Firewalls are one of the foundational technologies in network security. A firewall is a network security device that monitors, and controls incoming and outgoing network traffic based on predetermined security rules. It acts as a barrier between an organization's internal network and the external network, such as the internet. The primary purpose of a firewall is to prevent unauthorized access to the organization's network and protect against malware and other cyber threats.

There are several types of firewalls, including packet-filtering firewalls, stateful firewalls, application-level gateways, and next-generation firewalls. Each type of firewall has its own set of features and capabilities, but they all share the same basic functions of monitoring and controlling network traffic.

1. **Packet-filtering firewalls** are the most basic type of firewall. They work by examining each packet of data that passes through the firewall and comparing it to a set of predefined rules. If the packet meets the criteria of the rule, it is allowed to pass through the firewall. If not, it is blocked.
2. **Stateful firewalls** are an advanced type of firewall that can track the state of a network connection. They can monitor the sequence of packets sent between two hosts and determine whether they belong to a valid

connection. Stateful firewalls are more effective than packet-filtering firewalls at preventing certain types of attacks, such as session hijacking.

3. **Application-level gateways**, also known as proxies, are another type of firewall. They work at the application layer of the network stack and can examine the contents of each packet, including the application data. Application-level gateways can provide more granular control over network traffic, but they can also introduce latency and slow down network performance.
4. **Next-generation firewalls (NGFWs)** are a newer type of firewall that combines the features of packet-filtering firewalls, stateful firewalls, and application-level gateways. NGFWs can inspect network traffic at the application layer, provide advanced threat protection, and integrate with other security technologies, such as intrusion detection and prevention systems (IDPS) and security information and event management (SIEM) systems.

In addition to the different types of firewalls, there are also different deployment models, including network-based firewalls and host-based firewalls.

Deployment models of Firewall

Firewalls can be deployed in different ways depending on the organization's security requirements and network architecture. The two most common deployment models for firewalls are network-based firewalls and host-based firewalls.

1. **Network-based Firewalls:** Network-based firewalls are deployed at the network perimeter, typically between an organization's internal network and the internet. They act as a gateway between the two networks and monitor all incoming and outgoing traffic to enforce the organization's security policies.

Network-based firewalls can be further classified into the following subtypes:

A. **Packet filtering firewalls:** These firewalls filter network traffic based on pre-defined rules. They examine each packet and compare it to the firewall rules before deciding whether to allow it through or not. Packet filtering firewalls are simple and effective, but they offer limited protection against advanced attacks.

B. **Stateful inspection firewalls:** These firewalls maintain the state of network connections and can track packets belonging to the same connection. They can identify suspicious packets that don't belong to a known connection and block them. Stateful inspection firewalls provide better protection than packet filtering firewalls against certain types of attacks, such as session hijacking.
C. **Application-level gateways or proxy firewalls:** These firewalls provide deep packet inspection and can examine the content of each packet at the application layer. They can filter traffic based on application-specific rules and protect against advanced threats such as malware and botnets.
D. **Next-Generation Firewalls:** These firewalls combine the features of the previous three types of firewalls and provide more advanced security capabilities, such as intrusion prevention, SSL decryption, and deep packet inspection.

2. **Host-based Firewalls:** Host-based firewalls are installed on individual devices such as servers, endpoints, and mobile devices to protect them from network-based attacks. Host-based firewalls can monitor incoming and outgoing traffic on the device and block malicious traffic. They are particularly useful for securing devices that are frequently on the move or outside the organization's network perimeter.

   Host-based firewalls can be further classified into the following subtypes:

A. **System-level firewalls:** These firewalls run on the operating system and can filter traffic based on port numbers, protocols, and IP addresses.
B. **Application-level firewalls:** These firewalls provide granular control over network traffic by filtering traffic based on application-specific rules. They can also monitor application behaviour and block malicious actions.

In summary, network-based firewalls are deployed at the network perimeter to protect the organization's internal network from external threats, while host-based firewalls are installed on individual devices to protect them from network-based attacks. Both deployment models have their advantages and disadvantages and can be used together to provide a layered defence against cyber threats.

Firewalls are a critical component of network security, but they are not foolproof. Attackers can bypass firewalls through various means, such as exploiting vulnerabilities in the firewall software or using social engineering to trick users into opening malicious attachments or clicking on links. It's important to implement a comprehensive security strategy that includes multiple layers of defense and continuous monitoring to detect and respond to potential security incidents.

Network Access Control (NAC)

Network Access Control (NAC) is a security solution that regulates access to network resources by enforcing security policies. NAC solutions are designed to ensure that only authorized and compliant devices are allowed access to an organization's network resources, while unauthorized or non-compliant devices are denied access or placed in a quarantined area where they can be remediated.

NAC solutions typically work by inspecting devices that attempt to connect to the network and enforcing security policies based on the device's compliance status. NAC solutions can use a variety of techniques to identify devices, such as MAC address, IP address, and device certificates.

Once a device is identified, the NAC solution can perform a compliance check to ensure that the device meets the organization's security policies. Compliance checks can include verifying that the device has up-to-date antivirus software, that the operating system is patched, and that the device is not running unauthorized software.

If the device passes the compliance check, it is granted access to the network resources. If the device fails the compliance check, it is either denied access or placed in a quarantined area where it can be remediated.

NAC solutions can be deployed in different ways, including:

1. **Agent-based NAC**: In this deployment model, software agents are installed on devices to perform compliance checks and enforce security policies. Agent-based NAC solutions provide granular control over network access and can perform detailed compliance checks, but they can be difficult to deploy and manage, especially in large environments.

2. **Agentless NAC:** In this deployment model, compliance checks are performed without the need for software agents. Instead, the NAC solution uses network-based techniques such as DHCP snooping, ARP inspection, and port security to identify and control network access. Agentless NAC solutions are easier to deploy and manage than agent-based solutions, but they may not provide the same level of control and granularity.
3. **Hybrid NAC:** In this deployment model, both agent-based and agentless techniques are used to perform compliance checks and control network access. Hybrid NAC solutions provide the benefits of both agent-based and agentless solutions, but they can be more complex to deploy and manage.

In summary, NAC is a security solution that regulates access to network resources by enforcing security policies based on device compliance status. NAC solutions can be deployed in different ways, and each deployment model has its advantages and disadvantages. NAC solutions are an important part of an organization's security strategy, as they help to prevent unauthorized access to network resources and reduce the risk of data breaches.

Intrusion Prevention and Detection System (IPDS)

Intrusion Prevention System (IPS) and Intrusion Detection System (IDS) are two critical security solutions that help protect networks and systems from security threats. While both systems are designed to detect and prevent security incidents, they do so in different ways.

1. **Intrusion Detection System (IDS)** is a passive security system that monitors network traffic and system activity for signs of suspicious or malicious activity. IDS works by analyzing network traffic and looking for patterns that indicate a security breach, such as unusual login activity, unauthorized access attempts, or anomalous traffic patterns. When IDS detects a potential security threat, it generates an alert and notifies the security team, allowing them to investigate and respond to the threat.

IDS does not actively block or prevent security threats from occurring. Instead, it serves as an early warning system, alerting the security team to potential security incidents so that they can take appropriate action.

2. **Intrusion Prevention System (IPS)** is an active security system that not only detects but also actively prevents security incidents from occurring. IPS works by analyzing network traffic in real-time and looking for patterns that indicate a security threat. When IPS detects a potential security threat, it takes immediate action to block or prevent the threat from reaching its target.

IPS can take a variety of actions to prevent security threats, such as blocking network traffic from suspicious IP addresses, blocking access attempts from unauthorized users, or dropping malicious packets. IPS can be configured to operate in different modes, such as inline mode, where all network traffic is inspected and blocked or allowed based on the security policy, or passive mode, where IPS operates in monitoring mode and alerts are generated when a security threat is detected.

IPS and IDS are often used together as part of a layered security approach, where IDS provides early warning of potential security threats, and IPS takes immediate action to prevent the threats from reaching their target. The use of both IPS and IDS can help organizations to improve their overall security posture, reduce the risk of security incidents, and mitigate the impact of security breaches when they do occur.

Virtual Private Networks and Its security

A Virtual Private Network (VPN) is a technology that allows users to securely connect to a private network from anywhere over the public internet. VPNs use encryption to create a secure and private connection between the user's device and the network. This allows users to access network resources as if they were physically present within the network, even when they are located outside the network.

VPN is typically used by organizations to allow their employees to securely access network resources while working remotely. VPN can also be used by individuals who want to protect their online privacy and security while browsing the internet. When a user connects to a VPN, their internet traffic is routed through the VPN server, which encrypts the traffic and masks the user's IP address. This makes it difficult for third parties to intercept the user's internet traffic or track their online activities.

Types of VPN

There are two main types of VPN:

1. **Remote Access VPN:** Remote access VPN allows remote users to connect to a private network securely over the internet. Remote users can use a VPN client on their device to establish a secure connection to the VPN server, which then provides access to the network resources.
2. **Site-to-Site VPN:** Site-to-site VPN allows two or more networks to securely communicate with each other over the public internet. This is typically used by organizations with multiple locations or branch offices that need to share resources or communicate securely with each other.

VPN Security

VPN is an essential technology for remote access and has become more critical in recent years with the rise of remote work. VPN security is of utmost importance to ensure that sensitive data is protected from unauthorized access or interception by third parties. Here are some critical aspects of VPN security:

1. **Encryption:** VPNs use encryption to ensure that data transmitted between the remote user and the network is protected from interception by unauthorized parties. The two most commonly used VPN encryption protocols are SSL/TLS and IPsec.
2. **Authentication:** VPN authentication ensures that only authorized users can access the network. Typically, this involves the use of a username and password, or more robust authentication mechanisms such as multifactor authentication.
3. **Access Control:** Access control is used to restrict remote user access to specific network resources based on their level of authorization. This can include limiting access to sensitive data or specific applications.
4. **Logging and Auditing:** VPNs should log all access and activity on the network to detect any unauthorized access attempts or suspicious

activity. Regular auditing of VPN logs is necessary to ensure that the network is secure and that any breaches are detected and addressed promptly.

5. **Endpoint Security:** VPN endpoint security is critical to ensure that remote user devices are secure and free from malware or other security threats. This can involve implementing endpoint protection software or requiring remote users to adhere to strict security policies and best practices.

Overall, VPN security is a critical aspect of any organization's cybersecurity strategy, particularly for those with a remote workforce. Ensuring that VPNs are secure and properly configured can go a long way in protecting sensitive data and preventing security breaches.

VPN is a critical technology for remote access and has become more important in recent years with the rise of remote work. VPN provides a secure and private connection to network resources over the public internet, making it an essential tool for organizations and individuals alike.

Network security in cloud

Network security in the cloud is an important consideration for organizations that are moving their data and applications to the cloud. Cloud computing offers many benefits, including scalability, flexibility, and cost savings, but it also introduces new security challenges that must be addressed. Network security in the cloud is concerned with protecting the communication channels and data flows between cloud services, applications, and end-users.

Here are some key network security considerations for the cloud:

6. **Secure Network Architecture:** A secure network architecture is the foundation for network security in the cloud. This includes designing a secure network topology, implementing secure protocols, and using firewalls and other security measures to control network traffic.
7. **Identity and Access Management:** Identity and access management (IAM) is a critical aspect of network security in the cloud. IAM solutions should be used to manage user identities, control access to cloud resources, and enforce strong authentication and authorization policies.

8. **Data Encryption:** Data encryption is an important security measure in the cloud. Data should be encrypted both in transit and at rest to protect against interception or unauthorized access. Cloud providers offer encryption services that can be used to protect data.
9. **Network Monitoring:** Network monitoring is essential to detect and respond to security threats in the cloud. This includes monitoring network traffic, log files, and other sources of data to detect any anomalies or suspicious activity.
10. **Disaster Recovery:** Disaster recovery is an important consideration for network security in the cloud. Organizations should have a disaster recovery plan in place to ensure that data can be recovered in the event of a security breach or other disaster.
11. **Compliance:** Compliance with industry and government regulations is an important consideration for network security in the cloud. Organizations must ensure that their cloud deployments meet regulatory requirements and that data is protected according to industry standards.

Overall, network security in the cloud is a complex and challenging area that requires careful planning and execution. Organizations must work closely with their cloud providers to ensure that their cloud deployments are secure and that their data is protected from threats.

Conclusion

Network security is critical for protecting an organization's digital perimeter and ensuring business continuity. By implementing key technologies and best practices, organizations can help prevent unauthorized access, protect against cyber threats, and maintain the confidentiality, integrity, and availability of their network resources. As cyber threats continue to evolve, it's crucial to stay vigilant and continually assess and update your network security measures to ensure they remain effective.

V

Application Security & Mobile Security

Introduction

Application security refers to the measures taken to protect software applications from cyber-attacks, including the unauthorized access, modification, or destruction of sensitive data. Application security and Mobile Security is important because many cyber-attacks target vulnerabilities in software applications to gain access to valuable data or to disrupt business operations. In this chapter, we will discuss the key aspects of application security, including common application security threats, best practices for securing applications, and techniques for testing and auditing application security.

Common Application Security Threats

There are many common application security threats that organizations need to be aware of, including:

1. **Injection Attacks:** Injection attacks occur when malicious code is injected into an application in order to exploit vulnerabilities in the code. This can result in unauthorized access to sensitive data or the modification or destruction of data.

2. **Cross-Site Scripting (XSS):** XSS attacks occur when an attacker injects malicious code into a web page viewed by other users. This can result in the theft of sensitive data or the unauthorized access to a user's account.
3. **Cross-Site Request Forgery (CSRF):** CSRF attacks occur when an attacker sends a request to an application from a user's browser without their knowledge or consent. This can result in unauthorized actions being taken on behalf of the user.
4. **Broken Authentication and Session Management:** Broken authentication and session management occur when an attacker gains access to a user's account or session by exploiting vulnerabilities in the authentication and session management mechanisms.
5. **Malware:** Malware refers to any malicious software that is designed to exploit vulnerabilities in an application or operating system. This can result in the theft of sensitive data or the unauthorized access to a user's account.

Injection Attacks

Injection attacks are a type of security vulnerability that occurs when an attacker is able to insert malicious code or data into an application or system. The goal of an injection attack is typically to trick the application or system into executing unintended actions, such as disclosing sensitive information or performing unauthorized operations.

There are several types of injection attacks, including SQL injection, command injection, and XML injection.

1. **SQL Injection:** SQL injection attacks occur when an attacker is able to insert malicious SQL statements into an application's database query. The attacker may be able to gain unauthorized access to the database or to retrieve sensitive information.
2. **Command Injection:** Command injection attacks occur when an attacker is able to inject malicious code into a command that is executed by an application or system. The attacker may be able to execute arbitrary commands on the system or to gain unauthorized access to sensitive information.
3. **XML Injection:** XML injection attacks occur when an attacker is able to inject malicious XML code into an application's input data. The attacker

may be able to execute arbitrary code on the system or to retrieve sensitive information.

Preventing injection attacks involves a number of best practices, such as validating input data, using prepared statements or parameterized queries, and using input filters or firewalls to block malicious code. Additionally, developers should always be aware of the potential for injection attacks and should take steps to minimize their impact on the system.

Cross-Site Scripting (XSS) Attacks

Cross-Site Scripting (XSS) is a type of web application vulnerability where an attacker injects malicious code into a web page viewed by other users. This code is usually in the form of a script written in JavaScript or HTML and can be used to steal sensitive user information or perform unauthorized actions on behalf of the user.

There are two main types of XSS attacks: Reflected and Stored.

1. **Reflected XSS**: Reflected XSS attacks occur when an attacker injects malicious code into a URL or input field, which is then reflected back to the user's browser in the response from the server. When the user clicks on the link or submits the form, the malicious code executes, giving the attacker access to sensitive information or control over the user's session.
2. **Stored XSS**: Stored XSS attacks occur when an attacker is able to inject malicious code into a website's database, which is then displayed to all users who view the affected page. This type of attack can be especially dangerous, as it can affect multiple users and persist even after the initial attack is removed.

Preventing XSS attacks involves a number of best practices, such as encoding user input, filtering or blocking dangerous characters, and using security libraries or frameworks. Additionally, users should be educated on how to recognize and avoid potential XSS attacks, such as by avoiding clicking on suspicious links or entering sensitive information into untrusted websites.

Testing and Auditing Application Security

Testing and auditing are important components of application security. There are several techniques that can be used to test and audit application security, including:

1. Security Audits: Security audits involve reviewing the security controls and processes in place to ensure that they are effective in protecting the application and its data.
2. Vulnerability Scanning: Vulnerability scanning involves using automated tools to scan an application for known vulnerabilities.
3. Penetration Testing: Penetration testing involves simulating an attack on an application to identify vulnerabilities and weaknesses.
4. Code Review: Code review involves reviewing the source code of an application to identify vulnerabilities and weaknesses.

Best Practices for Securing Applications

There are many best practices that organizations can follow to secure their applications, including:

1. Secure Coding Practices: Developers should follow secure coding practices when writing applications, including input validation, error handling, and access control.
2. Authentication and Access Control: Applications should use strong authentication and access control mechanisms to ensure that only authorized users have access to sensitive data.
3. Encryption: Sensitive data should be encrypted both in transit and at rest to protect against unauthorized access.
4. Patch Management: Applications should be regularly patched to ensure that any known vulnerabilities are addressed.
5. Network Security: Applications should be protected by firewalls and other network security measures to prevent unauthorized access.
6. User Education: Users should be educated about common application security threats and how to protect their accounts and data.

Vulnerability Assessment and Penetration Testing

Vulnerability Assessment and Penetration Testing (VAPT) is a comprehensive security testing approach used to identify and mitigate security vulnerabilities in an organization's information systems. VAPT combines the strengths of both vulnerability assessments and penetration testing to provide a more complete understanding of an organization's security posture.

Vulnerability Assessment: Vulnerability assessment is the process of identifying vulnerabilities and weaknesses in an organization's information systems, including servers, applications, and network infrastructure. This is typically done through the use of automated tools, which scan for known vulnerabilities and weaknesses. The goal of a vulnerability assessment is to identify potential areas of weakness that could be exploited by an attacker.

Penetration Testing: Penetration testing is the process of simulating an actual attack on an organization's information systems. This is done by attempting to exploit identified vulnerabilities in a controlled manner, to see how far an attacker could get and what sensitive data they could access. The goal of penetration testing is to identify potential weaknesses that may not have been detected during a vulnerability assessment.

A Vulnerability Assessment and Penetration Testing engagement typically involves the following steps:

1. **Scoping:** defining the scope of the engagement, including the systems to be tested and the testing methodology.
2. **Reconnaissance:** gathering information about the target systems, including IP addresses, open ports, and potential vulnerabilities.
3. **Vulnerability assessment:** using automated tools to scan for known vulnerabilities and weaknesses in the target systems.
4. **Penetration testing:** attempting to exploit identified vulnerabilities in a controlled manner, to see how far an attacker could get and what sensitive data they could access.
5. **Reporting:** documenting the findings of the engagement, including identified vulnerabilities, recommended remediation steps, and overall risk assessment.

VAPT is an important component of any organization's security program, as it helps to identify and mitigate potential security risks before they can be exploited by attackers.

Application Security tools

Application security tools are used to identify vulnerabilities and secure applications against attacks. These tools can be classified into different categories based on their purpose and functionality. Some common categories of application security tools are:

1. Static Application Security Testing (SAST) Tools: SAST tools are used to analyze the application's source code for potential security vulnerabilities. These tools can identify vulnerabilities such as buffer overflows, injection flaws, and authentication issues.
2. Dynamic Application Security Testing (DAST) Tools: DAST tools are used to test the application's functionality while it is running. These tools can identify vulnerabilities such as cross-site scripting (XSS) and SQL injection.
3. Interactive Application Security Testing (IAST) Tools: IAST tools combine the features of both SAST and DAST tools. They can analyze the source code and provide real-time feedback while the application is running.
4. Web Application Firewall (WAF) Tools: WAF tools are used to protect web applications from attacks such as XSS, SQL injection, and cross-site request forgery (CSRF). These tools can monitor incoming traffic and block requests that are deemed malicious.
5. Penetration Testing Tools: Penetration testing tools are used to simulate attacks on the application to identify vulnerabilities. These tools can simulate attacks such as SQL injection, cross-site scripting, and file inclusion attacks.
6. Code Review Tools: Code review tools are used to analyze the application's source code for potential security vulnerabilities. These tools can identify vulnerabilities such as buffer overflows, injection flaws, and authentication issues.
7. Configuration Management Tools: Configuration management tools are used to manage and automate the configuration of the application environment. These tools can ensure that the application is configured securely and in compliance with security standards.
8. Dependency Management Tools: Dependency management tools are used to manage the application's dependencies and ensure that they are up-to-date and secure.

Application security tools are essential for securing applications against attacks. By using a combination of these tools, organizations can identify and address potential vulnerabilities, reducing the risk of attacks and protecting their systems and data.

Key Considerations for Effective Application Security:

The Key Considerations for effective application security are given below:

1. **Comprehensive Application Security Strategy:** A comprehensive application security strategy is essential to ensure that the applications used by an organization are secure and resilient to attacks. This strategy should include processes and tools to identify and mitigate vulnerabilities in applications during all stages of the development life cycle. The strategy should cover the complete application stack, including the underlying infrastructure and data sources, and should take into consideration the unique security requirements of each application.
2. **Policies and Procedures:** Policies and procedures are a critical component of application security. These documents provide clear guidelines for developers, testers, and other stakeholders on how to develop and maintain secure applications. Policies and procedures should cover all aspects of the application development life cycle, including requirements gathering, design, coding, testing, deployment, and maintenance. The policies and procedures should also include guidelines for managing security incidents and breaches.
3. **User Education and Awareness:** User education and awareness are critical to the success of any application security strategy. Users are often the first line of defense against attacks and must be educated on how to identify and respond to potential security threats. This includes providing training on how to recognize phishing emails, how to use secure passwords, and how to identify and report suspicious activity.
4. **Incident Response Planning in Application Security:** An incident response plan is an essential component of any application security strategy. This plan outlines the steps that should be taken in the event of a security breach, including who should be notified and what actions should be taken to contain and mitigate the damage. The incident

response plan should be regularly reviewed and updated to ensure it remains relevant and effective.

5. **Continuous Improvement and Adaptation in Application Security:** Application security is an ongoing process that requires continuous improvement and adaptation to remain effective. Threats and vulnerabilities are constantly evolving, and application security strategies must be updated to address these changes. This includes regular vulnerability assessments, penetration testing, and code reviews to identify and address new vulnerabilities. Additionally, application security strategies should be evaluated regularly to ensure they align with the organization's evolving security needs and priorities.

A comprehensive application security strategy should include a range of policies, procedures, tools, and training to ensure that applications are developed, tested, and maintained in a secure manner. This strategy should be regularly reviewed and updated to remain relevant and effective in the face of evolving security threats and vulnerabilities.

Secure Software Development

Secure software development refers to the process of designing, developing, testing, and deploying software in a way that ensures it is secure and resilient to cyber-attacks. Secure software development is important because software vulnerabilities can be exploited by attackers to compromise the confidentiality, integrity, and availability of an organization's data and systems.

The following are some best practices for secure software development:

1. **Threat Modeling:** Threat modeling is the process of identifying potential security threats to a software system and analyzing how these threats can be mitigated. Threat modeling helps to identify potential vulnerabilities early in the development process, reducing the overall risk to the system.
2. **Secure Coding:** Secure coding involves writing code that is free from security vulnerabilities. This includes following secure coding best practices, such as input validation, error handling, and secure communication protocols.

3. **Testing:** Testing is an essential part of secure software development. It includes both functional and security testing, such as penetration testing and vulnerability scanning, to identify potential security weaknesses.
4. **Patch Management:** It is important to keep software up-to-date with the latest security patches to address newly discovered vulnerabilities. Regular patch management reduces the risk of exploitation by attackers.
5. **Access Controls:** Access controls are used to limit access to sensitive data and functions within the software system. Access controls can be implemented using role-based access control, permission-based access control, and other access control mechanisms.
6. **Encryption:** Encryption is used to protect sensitive data in transit and at rest. Data should be encrypted using industry-standard encryption algorithms to prevent unauthorized access.
7. **Incident Response:** It is important to have an incident response plan in place to address security incidents that may occur. This includes having a plan to identify, contain, and remediate security incidents, as well as a plan for communication and reporting.

Secure software development is essential for organizations to protect their systems and data from cyber threats. By following best practices for secure software development, organizations can reduce the risk of cyber-attacks and protect their systems and data from potential harm.

Mobile Application Security

Mobile applications have become an integral part of our daily lives, offering convenience and accessibility to various services. However, with the rise of mobile applications, there has also been a surge in security threats. Mobile application security refers to the measures taken to protect mobile applications from potential threats, such as data breaches, unauthorized access, and malware attacks.

Importance of Mobile Application Security

Mobile applications are vulnerable to security threats due to the vast amount of sensitive data they handle, including personal and financial information. A breach of this data can result in financial losses, identity theft, and reputational damage to both the user and the application provider. In addition, malicious actors can exploit vulnerabilities in mobile applications to gain unauthorized access to a user's device, infect it with malware, or steal data. Therefore, ensuring the security of mobile applications is crucial to protect user data and maintain the integrity of the application.

Steps to Ensure Mobile Application Security

1. **Secure Code Development Practices:** Developers must follow secure coding practices to create secure applications. This involves conducting a thorough risk assessment of the application to identify potential security threats and implementing appropriate measures to mitigate them. Additionally, developers should ensure that the code is free of vulnerabilities and follows the best practices of coding.
2. **Use of Encryption:** Encryption is an effective way of securing data transmitted between the user's device and the server. Mobile applications should use strong encryption algorithms to protect sensitive data, such as passwords and financial information, from unauthorized access.
3. **Secure Authentication:** Authentication is the process of verifying the identity of the user. Mobile applications should use secure authentication methods, such as two-factor authentication or biometric authentication, to ensure that only authorized users can access the application.
4. **Regular Security Testing:** Mobile applications should undergo regular security testing to identify vulnerabilities and threats. This includes conducting penetration testing and vulnerability scanning to identify weaknesses in the application's security.
5. **Regular Updates:** Mobile applications should be regularly updated to ensure that they are secure and up-to-date with the latest security patches. This includes both the application code and third-party libraries used in the application.
6. **User Education:** Users play a crucial role in ensuring the security of mobile applications. Users should be educated about the potential security threats and the steps they can take to protect their data, such as using strong passwords, avoiding public Wi-Fi, and installing anti-malware software.

Conclusion

Application security is an important component of overall cybersecurity. Organizations should follow best practices for securing applications, including secure coding practices, strong authentication and access control, encryption, patch management, and network security. Testing and auditing are also important components of application security and can help to identify vulnerabilities and weaknesses that need to be addressed. By taking a comprehensive approach to application security, organizations can protect their sensitive data and ensure that their applications are secure against cyber threats.

VI

Identity and Access Management

Introduction

In today's digital world, the security of data and systems is a major concern. Identity and Access Management (IAM) is an important aspect of Cybersecurity, which involves managing user identities and their access to resources. IAM ensures that only authorized users have access to sensitive information and resources while protecting them from unauthorized access.

IAM provides a framework that organizations use to manage user access to resources such as applications, databases, and files. In this chapter, we will discuss the various components of IAM, their importance, and how they work together to provide secure access to resources.

Components of IAM

IAM consists of three main components: Authentication, Authorization, and Auditing.

1. **Authentication**: Authentication is the process of verifying a user's identity before allowing them access to resources. It ensures that the user is who they claim to be. The authentication process includes various

methods such as passwords, biometric authentication, security tokens, and smart cards.

2. **Authorization:** Authorization is the process of granting or denying access to resources based on the user's identity and permissions. It ensures that users can only access the resources that they are authorized to access. Authorization can be based on the user's role, group membership, or specific permissions assigned to the user.
3. **Auditing:** Auditing is the process of monitoring and recording user activity to identify any unauthorized access attempts or suspicious behavior. Auditing allows organizations to detect security incidents and take appropriate action to prevent further damage.

IAM Architecture

IAM architecture consists of various components such as Identity Providers (IDP), Service Providers (SP), and User Directories

1. **Identity Providers (IDP)**: Identity Providers are responsible for authenticating users and providing identity information to Service Providers. IDPs are the primary source of user identities and provide a single sign-on (SSO) experience across multiple applications.
2. **Service Providers (SP)**: Service Providers are responsible for granting access to resources based on the user's identity and permissions. SPs use the identity information provided by IDPs to authenticate users and grant or deny access to resources.
3. **User Directories**: User Directories are repositories that store user information such as usernames, passwords, and permissions. User directories can be integrated with IDPs and SPs to provide a centralized IAM solution.

Importance and benefits of IAM in Cybersecurity

IAM is an essential component of cybersecurity because it helps to protect against unauthorized access to sensitive information. It also ensures that users have the appropriate level of access to the resources they need to perform their jobs.

The following are some reasons why IAM is important in cybersecurity:

1. Prevents Unauthorized Access: IAM ensures that only authorized users have access to sensitive information and resources, preventing unauthorized access.
2. Enables Compliance: IAM helps organizations comply with regulatory requirements, such as HIPAA and PCI-DSS, which require strict access controls and user authentication.
3. Simplifies Management: IAM simplifies the management of user accounts and access controls, making it easier to manage user access and monitor user activity.
4. Reduces Risks: IAM reduces the risks associated with unauthorized access, such as data breaches and insider threats.
5. Improved User Experience IAM provides a seamless user experience, allowing users to access multiple applications and resources with a single set of credentials.

Policies and Procedures in IAM

Policies and procedures play a critical role in IAM. They provide guidelines for managing user identities and access to resources. The following are some examples of policies and procedures that are commonly used in IAM:

1. Password Policies: Password policies establish guidelines for creating and managing passwords, including password complexity, length, and expiration.
2. Access Control Policies: Access control policies establish guidelines for managing user access to resources, including who is authorized to access specific resources and under what conditions.
3. User Account Management Procedures: User account management procedures provide guidelines for creating, modifying, and deleting user accounts.
4. Incident Response Procedures: Incident response procedures provide guidelines for responding to security incidents, including unauthorized access attempts and data breaches.

Best Practices for IAM

Implementing an effective IAM strategy requires a comprehensive approach that includes policies, procedures, and technology. Here are some best practices for implementing an effective IAM strategy:

1. Define access policies: Organizations should define clear policies and procedures for granting access to resources and data. This includes defining roles and permissions, as well as specifying the process for granting and revoking access.
2. Use strong authentication: Organizations should use strong authentication mechanisms, such as multifactor authentication, to ensure that only authorized users are accessing their systems.
3. Monitor and audit access: Organizations should monitor and audit user access to resources and data in order to detect and respond to potential security incidents.
4. Implement user provisioning and deprovisioning processes: Organizations should have processes in place for creating, updating, and deleting user accounts and permissions.
5. Train users: Organizations should provide training and education to users on the importance of IAM and how to properly use IAM tools and technologies.
6. Regularly review and update IAM controls: Organizations should regularly review and update their IAM controls to ensure that they are effective and up-to-date with current threats and technologies.

Conclusion

IAM is a critical component of cyber security that helps organizations protect their sensitive data and systems from unauthorized access. By implementing an effective IAM strategy that includes policies, procedures, and technology, organizations can reduce the risk of data breaches and improve their regulatory compliance and operational efficiency.

VII

Incident Response and Management

Introduction

In today's world, cybersecurity incidents have become more frequent and sophisticated, posing a significant threat to organizations of all sizes and industries. Therefore, incident response is a critical component of any organization's cybersecurity strategy. Incident response involves preparing for, detecting, responding to, and recovering from security incidents.

In this chapter, we will discuss the concept of incident response and its importance in cybersecurity. We will define what incident response is and why it is critical for organizations to have a solid incident response plan in place. Additionally, we will discuss various incident response frameworks, such as NIST, ISO, and SANS, and how they can help organizations prepare for, respond to, and recover from security incidents.

What is Incident Response

Incident response is a process that helps organizations detect, investigate, respond to, and recover from cybersecurity incidents such as data breaches, malware infections, and network intrusions. The incident response process typically involves a coordinated effort by various teams, including IT, security, legal, and management.

The primary goal of incident response is to minimize the impact of the incident, reduce downtime, and prevent further damage. An effective incident response plan can help organizations identify the root cause of the incident, contain and eradicate the threat, and recover systems and data to their pre-incident state.

Importance of Incident Response

Incident response is essential for organizations of all sizes and industries to protect their critical assets and reputation. In today's digital age, cyber threats have become more advanced, and organizations must be prepared to respond quickly and effectively to any incident.

An effective incident response plan can help organizations to:

1. Minimize the impact of the incident: Quick detection and response can help minimize the impact of the incident and reduce the risk of data loss or theft.
2. Prevent further damage: Rapid containment of the threat can help prevent further damage to the organization's network, systems, and data.
3. Improve recovery time: A well-designed incident response plan can help organizations recover systems and data to their pre-incident state quickly.
4. Enhance stakeholder trust: An effective incident response plan can help build stakeholder trust and maintain the organization's reputation.

Incident Response Frameworks

Various incident response frameworks are available to help organizations develop effective incident response plans. These frameworks provide a structured approach to incident response and help organizations prepare for, respond to, and recover from security incidents.

Some of the popular incident response frameworks include:

NIST Incident Response Framework

The National Institute of Standards and Technology (NIST) Incident Response Framework provides a structured approach to incident response that includes four phases: Preparation, Detection and Analysis, Containment, Eradication, and Recovery. The NIST framework is a comprehensive guide that helps organizations establish a strong incident response program that is flexible and scalable.

ISO 27035 Incident Management

The ISO 27035 Incident Management framework provides a structured approach to incident management that includes six phases: Preparation, Detection and Reporting, Assessment and Evaluation, Response, Investigation and Evidence Gathering, and Lessons Learned. The ISO 27035 framework is a comprehensive guide that helps organizations develop an effective incident management plan that aligns with the organization's business objectives.

SANS Incident Handling Process

The SANS Incident Handling Process provides a structured approach to incident handling that includes six phases: Preparation, Identification, Containment, Eradication, Recovery, and Lessons Learned. The SANS framework is a practical guide that helps organizations establish an effective incident response plan that is scalable and adaptable to various incident scenarios.

Incident Response Planning

Incident response planning is a critical process that helps organizations prepare for, detect, respond to, and recover from security incidents. In this section, we will cover the incident response planning phase, including the development of an incident response plan, the formation of an incident response team, and training and awareness for incident response.

Developing an Incident Response Plan

An incident response plan (IRP) is a documented, structured approach to handling security incidents. It outlines the steps that should be taken in the event of an incident and the roles and responsibilities of the incident response team. Developing an IRP involves the following steps:

1. Step 1: Define the scope - The scope of the IRP should be clearly defined, including the types of incidents it covers, the systems and assets it applies to, and the personnel involved.
2. Step 2: Identify key stakeholders - The stakeholders involved in incident response should be identified, including the incident response team,

executive management, legal, IT, and external partners.

3. Step 3: Conduct a risk assessment - A risk assessment should be conducted to identify potential threats and vulnerabilities, and determine the likelihood and impact of a security incident.
4. Step 4: Develop response procedures - Procedures for responding to various types of incidents should be developed, including incident reporting, containment, analysis, eradication, recovery, and documentation.
5. Step 5: Establish communication channels - Communication channels for incident reporting, escalation, and dissemination of information should be established.
6. Step 6: Review and test the plan - The IRP should be reviewed and tested regularly to ensure its effectiveness and identify areas for improvement.

Incident Response Team

An incident response team (IRT) is a group of individuals responsible for managing and responding to security incidents. The IRT should be composed of individuals with various skills, including technical expertise, communication, legal, and management.

The IRT should be trained and equipped to detect, investigate, contain, and resolve security incidents. The team should also have clear roles and responsibilities defined in the IRP, including incident coordination, technical analysis, legal compliance, and communications.

Training and Awareness

Training and awareness are critical components of incident response planning. The organization's personnel should be trained on the IRP, including their roles and responsibilities during an incident. Training should also cover incident detection and reporting, incident analysis and assessment, incident containment and eradication, and incident recovery and documentation.

Awareness programs should also be implemented to educate personnel on the current threat landscape, common attack methods, and best practices for preventing and responding to security incidents. This can include phishing simulations, cybersecurity awareness training, and incident response tabletop exercises.

Incident Identification and Triage

Incident Identification

The first step in incident response is to identify the incident. This can be done through various methods, such as network and system monitoring, security alerts, and reports from employees or customers. Incident identification is critical in order to respond quickly to the incident and minimize damage.

Network and system monitoring tools can be used to detect abnormal activity on the network or systems, such as unauthorized access attempts, malware infections, or data exfiltration. These tools can alert security teams to potential security incidents so that they can be investigated further.

Security alerts can also be generated by various security solutions, such as intrusion detection and prevention systems (IDS/IPS), firewalls, and antivirus software. These alerts can indicate a potential security incident and should be investigated promptly.

Reports from employees or customers can also be a valuable source of information for identifying security incidents. Employees or customers may report suspicious emails, phishing attempts, or other unusual activity that could indicate a security incident.

Incident Triage

Once an incident has been identified, it needs to be triaged. Incident triage involves assessing the severity and impact of the incident and prioritizing the response accordingly. Triage is important because it allows the incident response team to focus their efforts on the most critical incidents first.

The severity of an incident is typically determined by the potential impact on the organization. Incidents with a high potential for damage or disruption are considered severe, while incidents with a low potential for damage or disruption are considered minor.

The impact of an incident can be assessed by considering factors such as the scope of the incident, the data or systems affected, and the potential financial or reputational damage to the organization.

Incidents are typically triaged into three categories:

1. High: Incidents with a high potential for damage or disruption to the organization, such as a major data breach or ransomware attack.
2. Medium: Incidents with a moderate potential for damage or disruption to the organization, such as a minor data breach or a phishing attack on a single employee.
3. Low: Incidents with a low potential for damage or disruption to the organization, such as a minor policy violation or a single failed login attempt.

Communication and Notification

After an incident has been identified and triaged, it is important to communicate and notify the appropriate stakeholders. This includes internal stakeholders, such as senior management, IT teams, and legal teams, as well as external stakeholders, such as customers, partners, and regulators.

Communication and notification should be timely and accurate. Stakeholders should be provided with information about the incident, the potential impact, and the actions being taken to mitigate the incident. Effective communication can help to manage stakeholder expectations and minimize the potential damage to the organization.

Incident Containment and Eradication

After identifying and analyzing an incident, the next step in incident response is containment and eradication. This phase is critical in preventing the spread of the incident and minimizing damage to the organization. In this section, we will discuss various containment and eradication techniques and their importance in incident response.

Containment Strategies

Containment strategies are methods used to prevent the incident from spreading and minimize its impact on the organization. The following are some common containment strategies:

1. Isolation: Isolating affected systems or disconnecting compromised devices from the network can help prevent the incident from spreading to other systems.
2. Shutting down services: If the incident is affecting a specific service or application, shutting it down can help prevent further damage and give the incident response team time to investigate and remediate the issue.
3. Blocking traffic: Blocking traffic from known malicious IP addresses or domains can prevent the attacker from communicating with their command and control servers and limit their ability to control the compromised systems.
4. Implementing access controls: Implementing access controls, such as disabling user accounts or limiting access to sensitive data, can prevent the attacker from further compromising the organization's systems.

Eradication Techniques

Eradication techniques are methods used to remove the cause of the incident and restore systems to their previous state. The following are some common eradication techniques:

1. Removing malware: If the incident involves malware, the first step is to remove the malware from the affected systems. This can be done by using anti-virus software or by manually removing the malware.
2. Patching vulnerabilities: If the incident is caused by a vulnerability, the affected systems should be patched as soon as possible to prevent the attacker from exploiting the same vulnerability in the future.
3. Restoring data from backups: If the incident involves data loss, restoring the data from backups can help bring the systems back to their previous state.

Evidence Collection and Preservation During the containment and eradication phase, it is important to collect and preserve evidence for future analysis and legal purposes.

The following are some best practices for evidence collection and preservation:

1. Document all actions taken: All actions taken during the containment and eradication phase should be thoroughly documented, including the time and date of each action.
2. Collect volatile data: Volatile data, such as running processes and open network connections, should be collected before shutting down affected systems.
3. Use forensically sound methods: Forensically sound methods should be used when collecting and analyzing evidence to ensure the integrity and authenticity of the evidence.
4. Store evidence securely: The collected evidence should be stored securely to prevent tampering or destruction.

Incident Investigation and Analysis

This phase involves determining the cause and extent of the incident and collecting evidence for further investigation. It is a critical step in the incident response process as it helps organizations prevent future incidents and improve their security posture.

1. Root Cause Analysis

The first step in incident investigation and analysis is to conduct a root cause analysis. This process involves identifying the underlying cause of the incident and determining how it occurred. Root cause analysis can help organizations prevent similar incidents in the future by addressing the root cause.

2. Forensic Analysis

Forensic analysis is another important part of incident investigation and analysis. It involves the collection, preservation, and analysis of digital evidence related to the incident. Forensic analysis can help organizations identify the source of the attack and the extent of the damage caused. This information can be used to improve security controls and prevent similar incidents in the future.

3. Assessing Impact and Risk

Assessing the impact of the incident is also an important part of incident investigation and analysis. This involves identifying the systems and data that were affected by the incident and determining the extent of the damage. It also involves assessing the potential risk to the organization, such as financial loss, reputational damage, and regulatory non-compliance.

4. Reporting and Documentation

Finally, incident investigation and analysis involves reporting and documentation. This includes documenting the incident and its impact, as well as the steps taken to investigate and mitigate the incident. Reporting and documentation can help organizations comply with regulatory requirements and provide a record of the incident for future reference.

Incident Recovery and Remediation

Incident recovery and remediation are crucial components of the incident response process. Once the incident has been contained and the scope and impact of the incident have been assessed, the organization must begin the process of recovering and remediating affected systems and data.

Following steps are involved in Incident Recovery and Remediation:

1. Planning for Incident Recovery and Remediation Effective planning is essential for successful incident recovery and remediation. During the planning phase, the incident response team should develop a detailed plan for restoring affected systems and data and remediating any vulnerabilities that contributed to the incident. The plan should include the following:
2. Prioritization of Systems and Data: The incident response team should prioritize systems and data based on their criticality and the impact of the incident. The team should focus on restoring critical systems and data first, followed by less critical systems and data.
3. Restoration Strategy: The team should develop a strategy for restoring systems and data. This strategy should include procedures for restoring systems and data from backups, rebuilding systems, and reinstalling software and applications.
4. Vulnerability Remediation: The team should develop a plan for identifying and remediating vulnerabilities that contributed to the

incident. This may involve patching systems, updating software and applications, or implementing additional security controls.

5. Communication: The team should develop a communication plan for keeping stakeholders informed about the progress of the recovery and remediation process.
6. Execution of Incident Recovery and Remediation Once the incident recovery and remediation plan has been developed, the incident response team can begin executing the plan. The following steps should be taken:
7. Restoration of Systems and Data: The team should begin restoring critical systems and data first, followed by less critical systems and data. The team should follow the procedures outlined in the restoration strategy.
8. Vulnerability Remediation: The team should identify and remediate vulnerabilities that contributed to the incident. This may involve patching systems, updating software and applications, or implementing additional security controls.
9. Testing and Verification: Once systems and data have been restored and vulnerabilities have been remediated, the team should test and verify the integrity of the systems and data. This may involve conducting vulnerability scans, penetration testing, or other forms of testing to ensure that the systems and data are secure.
10. Communication: The team should keep stakeholders informed about the progress of the recovery and remediation process.
11. Testing and Verification After incident recovery and remediation, the incident response team should conduct testing and verification to ensure that the systems and data are secure. This may involve conducting vulnerability scans, penetration testing, or other forms of testing to identify any remaining vulnerabilities. The team should also verify that the restored systems and data are functioning properly and that there is no loss or corruption of data.

Incident Reporting and Documentation

Incident reporting and documentation are critical components of incident response. Organizations must ensure that they report and document all security incidents accurately and efficiently.

Incident Reporting

Reporting security incidents is essential for organizations to comply with legal and regulatory requirements. Reporting can also help the organization identify the root cause of the incident and take appropriate measures to prevent similar incidents from occurring in the future. The reporting requirements for security incidents may vary depending on the nature of the incident and the industry in which the organization operates.

The incident response team should have a clear understanding of the reporting requirements for security incidents. The team should also have a process in place for reporting security incidents to the appropriate authorities, such as law enforcement, regulatory bodies, and customers.

Incident Documentation

Documentation is an essential aspect of incident response. Documentation can help the organization keep track of the incident response process, record all actions taken during the incident, and create a record for legal and regulatory compliance purposes. Documentation can also help the organization improve its incident response process by identifying areas that require improvement.

The incident response team should create a detailed report documenting the incident response process. The report should include the following information:

1. A description of the incident, including the date, time, and location of the incident
2. The impact of the incident on the organization, including any data loss or downtime
3. The response actions taken by the incident response team, including containment, eradication, investigation, and recovery
4. The root cause of the incident, including any vulnerabilities or weaknesses in the organization's security systems
5. Lessons learned from the incident and recommendations for improving the incident response process.
6. The incident response team should also document all evidence collected during the incident response process, including system logs, network

traffic logs, and forensic evidence. This documentation can be used for legal and regulatory compliance purposes and can also be helpful for future incident response efforts.

Post-Incident Review and Lessons Learned Post-incident review and lessons learned are critical aspects of incident response. Post-incident review involves evaluating the incident response process to identify areas that require improvement. The incident response team should conduct a post-incident review after every security incident to identify areas for improvement.

Lessons learned involve identifying specific actions that can be taken to improve the incident response process. These actions can include changes to policies, procedures, and technology solutions. The incident response team should document all lessons learned and make recommendations for improving the incident response process.

Incident Response Management and Optimization

Incident response is a continuous process, and organizations need to continuously improve and optimize their incident response plan to be effective in mitigating security incidents. Incident response management and optimization includes following:

1. **Management of the Incident Response Team**

Managing the incident response team is a critical aspect of incident response management. The incident response team should have a designated incident response manager who is responsible for managing and coordinating the team's activities. The incident response manager should have the authority to make decisions and allocate resources during an incident response.

The incident response manager should also ensure that the incident response team members have the necessary training and skills to perform their roles effectively. The team members should be cross-trained to handle different types of incidents, and they should have a clear understanding of their roles and responsibilities during an incident response.

2. **Process Improvement**

Process improvement is an essential aspect of incident response optimization. Organizations should conduct post-incident reviews to identify areas of improvement in the incident response process. The post-incident review should include an analysis of the incident response plan's effectiveness, the performance of the incident response team, and the tools and technologies used during the incident response.

Based on the post-incident review, organizations should update their incident response plan, policies, and procedures to incorporate the lessons learned. The updated incident response plan should include improvements to the incident response process, such as more effective incident detection and response strategies and better coordination between different teams.

3. **Continuous Monitoring and Incident Response Testing**

Continuous monitoring and incident response testing are critical for incident response optimization. Organizations should continuously monitor their systems and networks for security threats and vulnerabilities that could lead to a security incident. This monitoring can include threat intelligence, security alerts, and security assessments.

In addition to continuous monitoring, organizations should conduct regular incident response testing to ensure that the incident response plan is effective and efficient. Incident response testing can include tabletop exercises, simulated attacks, and penetration testing.

Legal and Regulatory Considerations

Incident response teams must not only focus on addressing the technical aspects of a security incident but also consider the legal and regulatory implications of the incident. It is crucial for organizations to understand and comply with the applicable laws and regulations related to incident response.

1. Privacy Laws: Privacy laws, such as the General Data Protection Regulation (GDPR) in the European Union and the California Consumer Privacy Act (CCPA) in the United States, impose strict requirements on the collection, use, and protection of personal data. In the event of a security incident that involves personal data, organizations must comply with the applicable privacy laws and notify affected individuals within

the required timeframe.

2. Data Breach Notification Laws: Data breach notification laws require organizations to notify individuals and regulators in the event of a data breach. These laws vary by jurisdiction, but typically require notification within a certain timeframe, depending on the severity of the breach. Failure to comply with these laws can result in significant fines and legal consequences.
3. Cybersecurity Regulations: Many industries are subject to cybersecurity regulations, such as the Payment Card Industry Data Security Standard (PCI DSS) for the payment card industry and the Health Insurance Portability and Accountability Act (HIPAA) for the healthcare industry. These regulations impose specific cybersecurity requirements and mandate incident response plans and procedures.
4. Cyber Insurance: Cyber insurance can provide financial protection for organizations in the event of a security incident. These policies typically cover costs related to incident response, such as legal fees, forensic analysis, and notification expenses. However, it is essential to carefully review policy terms and conditions to ensure that the coverage meets the organization's needs.
5. Legal Contracts: Legal contracts, such as service level agreements (SLAs) and vendor contracts, can also impact incident response. These contracts should specify the security requirements and incident response expectations for all parties involved, as well as the legal and financial consequences of non-compliance.
6. Legal and Reputational Consequences: Incidents that involve personal data or other sensitive information can result in legal and reputational consequences for organizations. In addition to fines and legal fees, incidents can damage an organization's reputation and result in a loss of trust from customers and stakeholders.

Conclusion

Cyber Security Incident Response and Management is a critical component of any organization's security posture. It involves preparing for and responding to security incidents in a timely and effective manner to minimize the impact on the organization. A well-designed incident response plan should consider all aspects of incident response, from detection and analysis to containment, eradication, and recovery. Organizations should regularly review and update their incident response plans, conduct regular training and testing, and maintain a strong incident response team. By adopting a proactive approach to incident response, organizations can better protect themselves from cyber threats and ensure business continuity in the face of an attack.

VIII

Cybersecurity Awareness and Training

Introduction

Cybersecurity has become a critical concern for organizations of all sizes, as the number and complexity of cyber threats continue to increase. The consequences of a cyber-attack can be devastating, including financial loss, damage to the organization's reputation, and loss of sensitive data. One of the most effective ways to reduce the risks associated with cyber threats is through cybersecurity awareness and training.

In this chapter, we will explore the importance of cybersecurity awareness and training for organizations. We will also discuss the different types of threats and vulnerabilities that organizations face and how awareness and training can help mitigate these risks.

Why is Cybersecurity Awareness and Training Important?

Cybersecurity awareness and training is essential for organizations because it helps employees understand the risks associated with cyber threats and how to prevent and respond to them. It is crucial to educate employees about the importance of cybersecurity and the role they play in protecting the organization's information and systems.

Without proper cybersecurity awareness and training, employees may not be able to recognize and respond to cyber threats, leaving the organization vulnerable to attack. Additionally, employees may inadvertently engage in behaviors that put the organization at risk, such as clicking on suspicious links or using weak passwords.

Effective cybersecurity awareness and training can help employees recognize and respond to threats and vulnerabilities, reducing the risk of a successful cyber-attack.

Building a Cybersecurity Awareness and Training Program

Following are the steps involved in building a comprehensive cybersecurity awareness and training program.

1. Needs Assessment: The first step in building a cybersecurity awareness and training program is to conduct a needs assessment. This involves identifying the areas of the organization that are most vulnerable to cyber threats and assessing the level of knowledge and awareness of employees about cybersecurity. A needs assessment may involve conducting surveys, interviews, and focus groups to gather information.
2. Develop Training Objectives: Once the needs assessment is complete, the next step is to develop training objectives. These objectives should be specific, measurable, achievable, relevant, and time-bound (SMART). The objectives should be tailored to the needs of the organization and the roles and responsibilities of employees.
3. Create Training Content: After the training objectives are identified, the next step is to create training content. The training content should be engaging, interactive, and relevant to the employees‘ roles and responsibilities. The content should cover topics such as phishing, malware, password management, and social engineering.
4. Delivery Methods: There are several methods for delivering cybersecurity awareness and training, including online training, classroom training, and simulations. Online training is an effective and convenient way to provide training to employees. Classroom training provides hands-on training and allows for interaction between the trainer and the trainees. Simulations provide a realistic scenario that employees can use to practice their cybersecurity skills.

5. Implementation: Once the training content and delivery methods are determined, the next step is to implement the training program. This involves scheduling training sessions, providing access to online training, and ensuring that all employees complete the required training.
6. Evaluation: After the training program is implemented, it is essential to evaluate its effectiveness. This involves measuring the employees' knowledge and awareness of cybersecurity before and after the training program. It is also important to evaluate the training content and delivery methods to identify areas for improvement.
7. Conclusion: Building a comprehensive cybersecurity awareness and training program is essential for organizations to mitigate the risks associated with cyber threats. The program should include a needs assessment, development of training objectives, creation of training content, delivery methods, implementation, and evaluation. The program should be regularly reviewed and updated to ensure that it remains relevant and effective.

Threat Awareness Training

Threat awareness training is an essential part of any cybersecurity awareness and training program. The goal of this training is to educate employees on the different types of threats they may encounter and to teach them how to identify and report these threats. In this section, we will discuss the importance of threat awareness training and the key elements of an effective program.

Why is Threat Awareness Training Important?

Threat awareness training is critical because employees are often the first line of defense against cyber attacks. Cybercriminals often use social engineering tactics to trick employees into providing access to sensitive data or systems. These tactics can include phishing emails, fraudulent phone calls, and malicious websites. By training employees to recognize these threats, organizations can significantly reduce the risk of a successful attack.

Another reason why threat awareness training is essential is that cyber threats are continually evolving. New types of attacks emerge regularly, and organizations must ensure that employees are up-to-date on the latest threats and how to protect against them.

Key Elements of a Threat Awareness Training Program A comprehensive threat awareness training program should cover the following key elements:

1. Types of Threats: The program should cover the various types of threats that employees may encounter, such as phishing, malware, social engineering, and ransomware attacks. Employees should understand the tactics used in each type of attack and how to recognize them.
2. Warning Signs: Employees should learn to identify warning signs of a potential attack. For example, in the case of phishing, employees should be trained to look for suspicious emails that contain typos, grammatical errors, or links to unfamiliar websites.
3. Reporting: Employees should know how to report a potential threat. The program should provide clear guidelines on how to report an incident, including who to contact and the steps to take in case of a suspected breach.
4. Best Practices: The program should cover best practices for protecting against cyber threats. This may include creating strong passwords, keeping software up-to-date, and avoiding suspicious websites and emails.
5. Regular Refreshers: As previously mentioned, cyber threats are continually evolving, and employees must stay up-to-date on the latest threats and best practices. A good threat awareness training program should include regular refreshers to reinforce training and provide updates on new threats.

Delivery Methods Threat awareness training can be delivered in various ways, including:

1. Online Training: Online training can be an efficient way to deliver threat awareness training to a large number of employees. These training programs can be customized to the organization's specific needs and can include interactive elements such as quizzes and simulations.
2. Classroom Training: Classroom training can be effective for small groups of employees or for specialized training sessions. In-person training allows for more interactive discussions and can provide a more personalized learning experience.

3. Simulations: Simulations can be an effective way to train employees on how to respond to specific threats. These simulations can replicate real-world scenarios and provide employees with practical experience in identifying and responding to threats.

Data Security and Privacy Training

Data security and privacy are crucial components of any organization's cybersecurity strategy. A data breach or unauthorized access to sensitive information can have severe consequences, including loss of revenue, damage to reputation, and legal and regulatory penalties. Therefore, it is essential to have a robust data security and privacy training program in place to educate employees on the proper handling of sensitive information.

Why Data Security and Privacy Training is Important?

Employees are the first line of defense against data breaches and cyberattacks. However, they are also the weakest link. According to a report by IBM, human error is the cause of 95% of security incidents. This is why it is critical to provide employees with data security and privacy training to reduce the risk of accidental or intentional data breaches.

Data security and privacy training can help employees:

1. Understand the value of sensitive data: Employees need to understand the value of sensitive data and the potential consequences of a data breach. They should be aware of the types of data that require protection, such as personal identifiable information (PII), financial information, and confidential business data.
2. Identify threats to data security: Employees need to be trained on how to identify potential threats to data security, such as phishing attacks, malware, and social engineering. They should know the warning signs of these attacks, such as suspicious emails or requests for personal information.
3. Use secure practices when handling data: Employees should be trained on best practices for handling sensitive data, including the use of strong passwords, encryption, and secure file sharing. They should also understand the importance of secure network connections and the risks associated with using public Wi-Fi or unsecured networks.

4. Report data breaches: Employees should know how to report data breaches or suspicious activity to the appropriate channels within the organization. They should be aware of the organization's incident response plan and the importance of reporting incidents promptly.

Best Practices for Data Security and Privacy Training

When designing a data security and privacy training program, there are several best practices to follow:

1. Conduct a needs assessment: Before developing the training program, conduct a needs assessment to determine the areas that require training. This can include assessing the risk of data breaches, analyzing employee behaviors, and identifying the types of data that require protection.
2. Develop clear training objectives: The training objectives should be clear, concise, and measurable. The objectives should be based on the needs assessment and aligned with the organization's goals and objectives.
3. Create engaging training content: The training content should be engaging and interactive to increase employee participation and retention. This can include videos, case studies, and simulations.
4. Deliver training through multiple channels: Employees have different learning styles, so it is essential to deliver the training through multiple channels, such as online training, classroom training, and webinars.
5. Reinforce training regularly: Data security and privacy training should be an ongoing process. Employees should receive regular training and reinforcement to ensure they remain up-to-date on the latest threats and best practices.

Incident Response Training

In today's world, where cyber threats are increasing day by day, it has become essential for organizations to have a comprehensive incident response plan in place. However, having a plan is not enough; it is equally important to train employees on how to execute the plan effectively. Incident response training is a critical aspect of cybersecurity awareness and training that aims to educate employees on how to handle security incidents promptly and efficiently.

Why is Incident Response Training Important?

Training employees on incident response helps to minimize the damage caused by a security incident. Employees who are trained on incident response procedures can detect and report incidents quickly, contain and mitigate the impact of incidents, and communicate effectively with stakeholders during and after an incident. Incident response training also helps organizations to comply with legal and regulatory requirements and maintain customer trust and reputation.

Key Components of Incident Response Training: The incident response training program should cover the following key components:

1. Incident Detection and Reporting: Employees should be trained to detect and report incidents promptly. They should know the signs of a security incident and the proper procedures for reporting them.
2. Incident Response Plan: Employees should be trained on the organization's incident response plan. They should know their roles and responsibilities during an incident and how to execute the plan effectively.
3. Incident Containment and Mitigation: Employees should be trained on how to contain and mitigate the impact of incidents. They should know how to isolate affected systems, shut down services, or disconnect compromised devices from the network.
4. Communication: Employees should be trained on how to communicate effectively during and after an incident. They should know how to provide updates to stakeholders, such as management, customers, and law enforcement, and what information should be shared.
5. Incident Response Testing: Incident response training should include tabletop exercises to test the effectiveness of the incident response plan. These exercises can help identify gaps in the plan and provide opportunities to improve the plan.

Delivery Methods for Incident Response Training

There are several delivery methods for incident response training, including:

1. Online Training: Online training is a cost-effective and convenient way to deliver incident response training to a large number of employees. Online training modules can be customized to the organization's specific incident response plan and can be accessed by employees anytime and

anywhere.

2. Classroom Training: Classroom training allows for more interactive and hands-on training. Employees can ask questions and participate in discussions and exercises. Classroom training is also an excellent opportunity to build relationships among employees and foster teamwork.
3. Simulations: Simulations can provide a realistic experience of an incident without the actual damage caused by a real incident. Simulations can be conducted online or in a classroom setting, and employees can practice their incident response skills in a safe environment.

Security Awareness for Remote Workers

The COVID-19 pandemic has led to a surge in remote work, and this trend is expected to continue. However, working from home introduces new security risks, and employees need to be aware of these risks and how to mitigate them.

The Risks of Remote Work Remote work presents a unique set of security risks. Employees may be using unsecured Wi-Fi networks or personal devices that lack the same security features as company-issued devices. Additionally, the physical security of remote work environments may be weaker than that of a traditional office, making them more susceptible to theft and other physical security breaches. Remote workers are also more likely to be targeted by phishing attacks, which can lead to data breaches.

Best Practices for Remote Work Security To minimize the risks associated with remote work, employees should follow certain best practices. Some of these best practices include:

1. Use a company-issued device: If possible, employees should use a company-issued device rather than their personal device. Company-issued devices have built-in security features that personal devices may lack.
2. Use a VPN: Employees should use a virtual private network (VPN) to encrypt their internet traffic and protect their online activity from prying eyes. A VPN can also protect against man-in-the-middle attacks when using public Wi-Fi.

3. Enable multi-factor authentication: Multi-factor authentication adds an extra layer of security to logins by requiring a second form of identification, such as a fingerprint or a code sent to a mobile device.
4. Secure home Wi-Fi: Employees should secure their home Wi-Fi network with a strong, unique password and enable WPA2 or WPA3 encryption. They should also ensure that their router is running the latest firmware.
5. Avoid public Wi-Fi: Employees should avoid using public Wi-Fi networks whenever possible. If they must use public Wi-Fi, they should use a VPN to encrypt their traffic.
6. Be cautious of phishing emails: Employees should be extra cautious of emails that ask them to click on a link or download an attachment, especially if it comes from an unknown sender. They should verify the legitimacy of the email by checking the sender's email address, hovering over the link to see the URL, and confirming with the sender if necessary.

Remote Work Security Awareness Training Remote workers should receive security awareness training that is tailored to their unique risks and challenges. The training should cover the following topics:

1. The risks associated with remote work and how to mitigate them
2. Best practices for securing home Wi-Fi networks and company-issued devices
3. How to use a VPN and enable multi-factor authentication
4. How to recognize and avoid phishing emails and other social engineering attacks
5. What to do in the event of a security incident or data breach
6. Conclusion Remote work is becoming increasingly popular, but it presents new security risks that employees need to be aware of. By following best practices and receiving appropriate security awareness training, remote workers can help protect themselves and their organizations from cyber threats.

Cybersecurity Policy and Compliance Training

Cybersecurity policies define the framework that guides an organization's cybersecurity strategy, and compliance refers to the adherence to specific regulations and standards. Employees are the first line of defense in protecting an organization's sensitive information and systems. Therefore, cybersecurity policy and compliance training is essential for employees to understand their roles and responsibilities and to ensure that they follow the organization's security protocols.

Importance of Cybersecurity Policy and Compliance Training

Cybersecurity policy and compliance training is vital for employees to protect sensitive data and systems from cyber attacks. It ensures that employees understand the organization's security protocols and adhere to them to minimize the risk of a security breach. Furthermore, compliance training is essential to ensure that employees follow regulatory requirements and industry standards. Failing to comply with these requirements can result in legal and financial penalties, which can be detrimental to the organization's reputation and financial stability. Therefore, an effective cybersecurity policy and compliance training program can prevent security incidents, reduce risks, and avoid penalties.

Developing a Cybersecurity Policy

Developing a cybersecurity policy is the first step in implementing an effective cybersecurity program. A cybersecurity policy should outline the organization's objectives, the scope of the policy, and the roles and responsibilities of employees in ensuring compliance with the policy. It should also define the rules and guidelines for the use of IT resources, including access controls, password management, and the use of personal devices. Finally, it should include guidelines for incident reporting and response.

Training Employees on Cybersecurity Policy and Compliance

The cybersecurity policy and compliance training program should educate employees on the importance of the policy, their responsibilities in complying with the policy, and the consequences of policy violations. Employees should also be trained on specific procedures, such as password management, data handling, and incident reporting. The training program should be tailored to the employee's role and level of access to IT resources. For example, employees with access to sensitive data should receive more in-depth training on data handling procedures and security protocols.

Training Delivery Methods

The delivery method of cybersecurity policy and compliance training can vary, depending on the organization's size, location, and resources. Some common delivery methods include online training, classroom training, and workshops. Online training is the most popular method due to its convenience, scalability, and cost-effectiveness. Classroom training and workshops provide more interaction and personalization, allowing for a deeper understanding of the policy and compliance requirements.

Measuring the Effectiveness of Cybersecurity Policy and Compliance Training

To ensure the effectiveness of cybersecurity policy and compliance training, the organization should conduct periodic assessments to measure the employees' understanding of the policy and compliance requirements. The assessments can take various forms, such as quizzes, surveys, and simulations. The results of the assessments should be analyzed, and appropriate actions should be taken to address any knowledge gaps or policy violations.

Continuous Learning and Improvement

Effective cybersecurity awareness and training programs require ongoing evaluation and improvement to ensure their relevance and effectiveness in protecting an organization from cyber threats.

Evaluating Training Effectiveness

One of the first steps in continuous learning and improvement is evaluating the effectiveness of existing training programs. This can be done in several ways, including:

1. Metrics and Data Analysis: Using metrics such as training completion rates, incident response metrics, and employee feedback to gauge the effectiveness of the training program.
2. Testing and Simulation: Conducting regular testing and simulation exercises to evaluate how well employees are able to apply what they learned in training in real-world situations.
3. Incident Analysis: Analyzing the root cause of incidents and whether they were caused by lack of training or employee error.
4. Employee Feedback: Gathering feedback from employees through surveys, focus groups, and other methods to determine what is working and what needs improvement.

Improving Training Programs

Once training effectiveness has been evaluated, the next step is to identify areas for improvement and implement changes to the training program. Some key steps in this process include:

1. Updating Training Content: Keeping training content up-to-date and relevant to current threats and trends in cybersecurity.
2. Adjusting Delivery Methods: Adapting training delivery methods to meet the needs of employees, such as offering online training modules or mobile-based training.
3. Offering Ongoing Training: Providing ongoing training to reinforce key concepts and keep employees up-to-date on emerging threats.
4. Incorporating Feedback: Using employee feedback to improve training content, delivery methods, and overall program effectiveness.

Staying Up-to-Date

Finally, staying up-to-date with emerging threats and trends in cybersecurity is critical to continuous learning and improvement. This can be done by:

1. Monitoring Threat Intelligence: Keeping track of emerging threats and vulnerabilities through threat intelligence feeds and other sources.
2. Industry Best Practices: Staying informed on industry best practices and standards for cybersecurity.
3. Attending Conferences and Training: Participating in cybersecurity conferences and training programs to learn about new threats and solutions.

Conclusion

In conclusion, cybersecurity awareness and training are critical components of a robust cybersecurity strategy. As technology continues to advance and become more integrated into our daily lives, the risk of cyber attacks and data breaches increases. It is essential that individuals and organizations understand the potential threats and take proactive measures to protect their information.

Effective cybersecurity awareness and training programs should cover a range of topics, including password management, phishing scams, social engineering, and malware protection. These programs should also be regularly updated to reflect new and emerging threats and technologies.

Investing in cybersecurity awareness and training not only helps to protect sensitive data and prevent financial losses, but it also helps to build a culture of security within an organization. By educating employees and promoting safe online practices, organizations can reduce the risk of cyber attacks and improve their overall cybersecurity posture.

Ultimately, cybersecurity is everyone's responsibility, and it is crucial to remain vigilant and informed to stay ahead of cyber threats. By prioritizing cybersecurity awareness and training, individuals and organizations can better protect themselves against cyber attacks and safeguard their information in today's digital world.

FINAL WORDS

This book has covered a wide range of topics related to cybersecurity. We started with an introduction to cybersecurity, including the different types of threats and major cyber incidents. Then we delved into the importance of cybersecurity frameworks, risk assessment and management, network security, application security, identity and access management, incident response and management, and cybersecurity awareness and training.

Throughout this book, we have emphasized the importance of cybersecurity in today's digital landscape. Cyber threats are constantly evolving, and it is essential for organizations to implement effective cybersecurity measures to protect their assets and data. By understanding the key components of cybersecurity frameworks, conducting regular risk assessments, implementing strong network and application security measures, and developing effective incident response plans, organizations can better safeguard against cyber threats.

We hope that this book has provided a comprehensive overview of cybersecurity and the tools and best practices that organizations can use to enhance their cybersecurity posture. As technology continues to advance and cyber threats become increasingly sophisticated, it is essential for individuals and organizations to stay vigilant and proactive in their cybersecurity efforts.

www.ingramcontent.com/pod-product-compliance
Ingram Content Group UK Ltd.
Pitfield, Milton Keynes, MK11 3LW, UK
UKHW021923190726
13853UKWH00002B/805